Unconventional Success!

UNCONVENTIONAL
SUCCESS!
THE BRAD LIEBER STORY

BRAD LIEBER

Library of Congress Control Number: 2025917463
Paperback: 978-1-958314-02-9
Hardcover: 978-1-958314-03-6
eBook: 978-1-958314-04-3

This book is dedicated to my beautiful wife and life partner, Janet Lieber. Without her, Bradley Lieber, Systems & Space Incorporated, successes and dreams would not have been fulfilled. Her support has not only shaped our professional journey but also enriched our personal lives.

Janet's encouragement has been instrumental in my personal growth and in the success of our business. She remains my constant source of support and my biggest fan.

I always thought "thankyou" was one word, but Janet taught me otherwise. My gratitude and appreciation are meaningful because I am blessed to direct that appreciation toward the person I deeply love.

Janet, I am profoundly grateful for your love and support. You are the love of my life, and I am blessed to have you by my side. Thank YOU, my love!

Brad

And to my children

Dana and Ryan,

To say that I am proud of you would be an understatement. No words can express what I feel for the two of you. Your respect for each other and for Mom and me goes beyond words.

From the time the two of you were just kids, throughout your lives, and into your adulthood, you have always been so good, so kind, and so respectful. It thrills me to see the love you show for each other and for all the members of our family.

Know that your mom and I are always there for the two of you. Love you to the moon and back.

Dad

Contents

Preface

Here I am, nestled in my cozy and inviting office, part of a 2,800-square-foot upstairs space with a golf studio and lounge. My office, a creative sanctuary, exudes a warmth that could rival Kevin Costner's upstairs retreat in the movie "Hidden Figures." This space, nestled within our bustling 17,800-square-foot building, is not just a workplace but a haven where creativity and camaraderie thrive. The walls are adorned with a delightful collage of commissioned paintings and cherished sports memorabilia, each imbued with its own unique story. Take, for instance, the Steelers jersey signed by the legendary "Steel Curtain": Joe Greene, L.C. Greenwood, Dwight White, and Ernie Holmes. Or those white Everlast boxing trunks signed by "The Greatest of All Time," Muhammad Ali—what a treasure! And then there's my "Hole-in-One" shadow box, a testament to that unforgettable day, signed by my fellow players Scott Archibald and Rich Gates.

A smile spreads across my face as I glance around at the thoughtfully arranged pieces of art hanging above the private cubicles on our first floor. Each piece is more than just decoration; it's a source of inspiration that ignites our passion for our business, reminding us of how we came together to program crucial deals and achieve our dreams. These pieces, with their vibrant colors and powerful imagery, serve as constant reminders of the creativity and potential that lie within us.

I remember the unexpected invitation from Garry Tramiel, son of Jack Tramiel, who in 1984 bought the Consumer Division of Atari Inc. from Warner Communications. He invited Janet and me to a private party at one of Carmel, California's beautiful Italian restaurants with a gathering of dignitaries and business owners. As I looked around, I couldn't help but wonder what I was doing there. Janet, I could understand—but me? It was a moment that left me both surprised and intrigued.

I was engaged in a late-night chat with a fella I'd met there, Sean Corrigan, President of Rockpoint Capital Ltd. We were swapping business stories, enjoying the food and fine wine. We were lost in each other's stories about the adventures and unexpected twists life had thrown at us. Out of the blue, Sean leaned in and said, "Brad, you need to write a book. You've got a story worth telling, my friend."

"Write a book? What on earth is he talking about?" I thought, a bit stunned. After all, I'd never finished high school. The thought seemed preposterous. "Get out of here." Yet, as that conversation replayed in my mind, the tiniest seed of possibility began to sprout.

What you are about to read is not your conventional *How to Become a Success* book. I didn't have an education—well, not a traditional education. I didn't read all the business books or the stories of other successful people's experiences. That was their story, their world. But I've realized the power of personal stories, and I believe mine is worth sharing.

I wasn't interested in a recipe for success—I wanted money and things. I wanted to do what I wanted to do, when I wanted to do it, with whoever could afford to do it with me. I wanted to have fun. In this pursuit of fun, I found my path to success, which was far from conventional but uniquely mine.

Then, it hit me: despite my life experiences, despite what others might have thought was lacking in my preparation, my life has soared beyond my wildest expectations, reaching heights I never dared to imagine!

Who knows? Maybe Sean was right. It may be time to tell my story.

Brad Lieber

Chapter 1
It's Just a Little Farther

November 7, 2024

I've known Alan Robinowitz all my life. He is my first cousin and, for the last sixteen years, my business partner in a clinic we established in January 2009. We've become closer as adults than we were as kids.

Alan's daughter, Aryn, was getting married, so Janet and I flew back to Pennsylvania to attend the wedding. (I'm a sucker for a party.) We landed at the Pittsburgh Airport, picked up our rental car, and proceeded to our hotel.

Driving along the highway, I noticed familiar signs: Lake Erie, Ashtabula, Cleveland, and Geneva-on-the-Lake. I thought, "This has to be close to Grand River Academy."

When we arrived at the Hampton Inn, I got our room key from the front desk and made our way to our room. I didn't even take the time to hang my clothes. I immediately checked my phone for Grand River's address.

Grand River Academy
3042 College Street
Austinburg, OH, 440-805-2090

I looked up the distance between Meadville, Pennsylvania, where we were staying, and Austinburg, Ohio.

"Hey, Janet. Ya know the prep school my dad sent me to? It's only about an hour from here."

Without hesitation, Janet said, "Let's go. Brad, you've got to go. It's only an hour away. Let's go. It's just a little farther."

I couldn't argue with her; after all, it was her suggestion. So, we set off for Austinburg.

I was filled with nervous anticipation and disbelief as we neared Grand River Academy. This was the place that had a significant impact on my life. Never did I think I would find myself returning there. Honestly, had I not succeeded, I would never have returned. It wasn't about bragging; I wanted to share with the educators that even the most challenging students can be positively impacted by their dedication, often without them even realizing it.

Truth be told, I didn't particularly like that school—though perhaps that's a bit harsh. I didn't like any school! What was the point? I just wanted to have fun. I wasn't asking for much; I wanted to enjoy myself, and most people I knew in Monessen weren't doing that. They might have enjoyed life when the steel mills operated, but after they closed? It was a ghost town, and so were the outlying cities. But that day, as I looked back, I could see the transformation from a rebellious student to a successful adult, and I couldn't help but feel a profound sense of pride.

It was a beautiful day, and we had a peaceful drive. The temperature was about sixty-five degrees, and the skies were clear. As we continued, we enjoyed the beautiful countryside I was beginning to remember.

It was just a little farther.

As we made our last turn, memories flooded my mind. My heart raced as I parked the car, and my palms were sweaty as I reached for Janet's hand. But amid the nervousness, there was also a palpable sense of joy and excitement.

"Oh, my God, Janet. Being here brings back so many memories." Janet just smiled. She intuitively knew this meant a lot to me and enjoyed every little-boy emotion I unintentionally exuded.

Holly Carper and Thomas Polk met us. I explained to them that I had been a student at Grand River Academy—actually, I had been a student a couple of times. I could tell they were interested, and we were welcomed with open arms.

Oddly, seeing Grand River was like seeing an old schoolmate. It had changed over the years, but in that moment, I was seeing it just as it had been fifty years before. I could picture the Buck brothers—Jeff, Rob, and my roommate, Mike—walking down the hall and giving me a knowing nod: "One day we'd get out!"

Then there were Tim Burke, Bud Fields, Joe Camelli, and Ron Ross, people I hadn't thought about for years. Suddenly, they were very much on my mind. I just wanted to see them and tell them, "Guys, I made it! Holy shit, I made it—ME!"

And there were many reasons to be surprised. Not that I was a bad kid. Grand River wasn't a reform school for delinquents. It was a school for wayward kids who just didn't fit into a conventional, regimented education—and didn't care. It was tailor-made for kids like me.

The memories were returning, flooding me with emotions as I tried to take them all in simultaneously. We walked down the hall into my dorm room. My attention was immediately focused on what had been in years past my window. It was still there. I had to chuckle. It was like a monument to my having passed through the doors and windows of Grand River Academy—twice!

Chapter 2
Early Education

On November 15, 1955, I became the third boy born to Herschel and Harriet Lieber. I was born in Pittsburgh, but we lived in Monessen. My elder brothers were twins, Robert (who we called Bob) and Steven (who went by Steve). The city of Monessen experienced significant growth during the rise of the steel industry. The Pittsburgh Steel Company, later renamed Wheeling-Pittsburgh Steel, employed most of the city's residents and those from the surrounding areas.

Life was simple back then, routine—*too* damned routine! The weight of societal expectations was heavy. You were expected to attend school, graduate, and secure a job at one of the three mills. Shortly after that, you would join the union, take a trip to Gibson Chevrolet, pick out a Monte Carlo, Chevelle, or Camaro, work for a year or two, marry your high school sweetheart, have dinner every night precisely at five o'clock, and retire to bed only to return to the steel mill the next day.

Monessen's Circle of Life was a unique rhythm, a predictable yet comforting pattern. It involved purchasing a tract home for ten to fifteen thousand dollars, enjoying drinks at the local bar, and retiring to live off your pension. Eventually, you would pass away, making room for the next group of prospective steelworkers who would follow in your footsteps. This was not just a routine, but a tradition, a way of life that had been passed down through generations. It was the way it was, the way it had always been in Monessen.

The Lieber family was not destined for the predictable path of the steel mill. In 1951, my grandfather, Isadore, established a flooring and furniture store in Donora, a Washington County, Pennsylvania, borough. The Lieber Furniture Store, located at 546-548 McKean Avenue, part of what was known as the Barone's Building, was more than just a business; it was a cornerstone of the community. At the same time, my grandmother on my mother's side, Gertrude Robinowitz, established Gertrude's Market, a butcher shop in McKeesport, Pennsylvania, further cementing our family's connection to their respective communities. They were not just smart; they were community-minded. They chose to serve the community of steelworkers, providing them with quality products and a personal touch, and in return, their businesses enjoyed support from the community.

Dad went to the University of Pittsburgh to become a doctor. Once there, he decided he'd rather make money. When my dad and his brother, my Uncle Jerry, took over the Lieber Furniture Store from my grandfather, they showed remarkable adaptability. They expanded the furniture portion while backing off on the flooring, understanding the changing market dynamics. The flooring didn't sell as quickly or as often as the furniture, and they were quick to adjust.

There I was, about to begin my education, and at this moment of my childhood, I was still happy. As a youngster, I eagerly anticipated our visits to Lieber Furniture with my grandfather. We'd walk down the alley on the opposite side of the street from Lieber's and through the alley door of Murphey's Five & Dime, where I'd always pick up a toy or a candy bar, adding to the thrill of our impending visit. Then we'd cross the street and enter my dad and uncle's furniture store, a place that always filled us with joy and excitement.

When my grandfather wasn't there to take me through Murphey's, my father took me to Costa's, the local coffee shop. It was a part of our morning routine, a comforting ritual. There, in the early morning, he'd join everybody to shoot the shit and catch up on what was happening in the community. Dad would buy me a crawler, which was an oblong donut topped with chocolate. The crawler and a carton of chocolate milk were the perfect breakfast.

I was too young at the time to realize it, but I was receiving my most impactful education. I would listen to my father's conversations with customers, hearing them tell him what they were looking for and watching him offer options they'd not considered. I'd witness the smiles, the exchange of money, the handshakes. It was a masterclass in success. These customers were friends. They knew my dad and knew he would do whatever it took to satisfy their needs. They could depend on him. These were not just customers; they were loyal patrons. Why would they ever consider shopping elsewhere? I was learning from the best.

With a diversified income instead of a single paycheck from the mill, my parents could afford a few nicer things. They built a custom home for around thirty-five thousand dollars on a development overlooking the Park Plan, a series of tract homes, and a shopping center. This was a step up, a move to a more exclusive area that reflected their hard work and success. Dad, an avid golfer, even had a golf membership at the Nemacolin Country Club in Belleville, Pennsylvania. This was a big deal, a symbol of their improved lifestyle and financial stability.

When I began vocational school, I was excited to make new friends. It would be an opportunity to have more fun and fill the boring gaps in activity that occasionally occur in a small community. The school only offered me the opportunity to sit still in my chair and follow the teacher's lesson plan. Even at a young age, I was uninterested in pursuing that opportunity.

I hated school. It wasn't my place. The teachers, whom I didn't know and who didn't know me, wanted to tell me what I had to do to get where I would someday want to be. They wanted me to conform and fit a mold. They didn't know what I wanted or where I was headed. I possessed a different kind of intelligence. I realized I was different at a young age. I was smart enough and aware enough to see the path that

others who had completed an education were on. They never appeared
happy. They never appeared to be having fun. I knew I didn't want to
be there. My vocational school grades were a reflection of my repeated
scholastic failures. I wasn't obstinate; I wasn't rebellious, and I certainly
wasn't dumb. I simply didn't care.

I did enjoy the Cub Scouts. I was eight years old when I joined
Cub Den 510. It was there that I made friends with Bob Gladys, and
his younger brother, Danny, who soon became my best buddy. We
nicknamed Danny "Dutch." I don't know why; it was just a nickname.
Dutch's mom was the Den Leader of Den 510. Her activities were fun,
and I never sensed that she was someone who was hovering critically
over me. What I felt was a sense of belonging. It's where I met many of
my first friends. Little did I know what a life-changing impact Dutch
would have on me.

As we grew older, Dutch became the school quarterback and a
talented athlete, while Cindy Sparacino, the head cheerleader, was his
perfect match. The three of us were very close friends, sharing a bond
that transcended our differences. They were my Gentile buddies, and
during the holidays, they allowed me to experience the best of both
worlds. I would have Christmas Eve dinner at one house and
Christmas morning breakfast at the other. Cindy's mom, Gilda, treated
me like I was her own, always encouraging and believing in me. Her
words, "Bradley, someday, someday," were a constant source of hope
and inspiration.

My vocational school teachers advanced me from grade to grade.
I'm not entirely sure why, except for the fact that most of the teachers
liked me—*most* of the teachers. There was one who did not: my sixth-
grade teacher, Miss Salotti. This lady was hot! I was infatuated with
her. I never listened to a word she said, but paying attention to her was
no problem for an eleven-year-old boy. Unfortunately, she couldn't
appreciate my uniqueness and charm.

As the end of the school year drew close, an impulse took hold of
me. Setting off a Fourth of July party popper during a quiet session in
our class would be fun for everyone. The last streamers were settling on

my desk when Miss Salotti, in a sudden burst of anger, exclaimed, "Bradley! I would flunk you for a nickel, but I don't want you here next year!"

Her outburst didn't bother me. We shared the same feelings. I didn't want to be there either. I wasn't the only one doing silly things; I was the only one who got caught. I was driven by a desire to have fun and see people happy. Mom's reaction was always the same: a mix of exasperation and understanding. "Oh, Bradley, you didn't do that, did you?" I was usually very honest, even when it got me into trouble. The thought of denying my actions never crossed my mind. Looking back, I realize it must have been doubly challenging for Mom. After all, she was a schoolteacher, too. But she always stood by me, her understanding and support never wavering.

I cared about school once every quarter: when report cards were issued. Like I said, I am usually very honest. I had enough brains and integrity to realize that changing my numerous F's to A's was inappropriate. I changed them to B's.

Mom and I were together when my teacher called to express concern over my grades. At first, it was difficult for Mom to understand. After all, I'd achieved almost all B's. But my teacher quickly explained that those B's were F's. The evidence was staring my mom and me in the face. I explained to my mom that I did not want to disappoint her or my dad. So, you see, I cared; I genuinely cared! However, I didn't care enough to bring my grades up.

Mom taught home economics and needlepoint. Our home was a magnet to all the neighboring kids. Mom always anticipated a flow of kids coming through the house and ensured everyone felt welcome. There was always a pot of soup on the stove for dipping bread, which was always empty by the time the kids left.

Speaking of pot. It wasn't just the pot of soup that my friends came to enjoy.

You have to understand that Monessen was bustling with business at one point in time, but there was very little to do for those of us who were younger. Our neighborhood was close-knit, and everyone knew each other and looked out for one another. I remember one time when I borrowed my dad's car.

Fern Shire, one of my mom's friends, called my mom and asked, "Is Bradley driving?"

My mother laughed and replied, "Why, no, Fern. Why do you ask?"

"I think I saw him driving down the street in your car," Fern explained.

Mom hung up the phone and looked out the window at the driveway. Our Plymouth Valiant was gone. I'd discovered that if you pushed the brakes and put the car in gear, you could turn the radio on and play music without the keys! This led me to the next level of self-education. I wanted to find out what else the car would do, but for that, I needed the keys. I wasn't stealing the car; it was ours. I just wanted to have fun —and it was fun until Fern Shire stuck her nose in my business.

People in positions of authority always wanted to ruin my attempts to enjoy life. I couldn't figure out why. It was none of their fucking business, and I wasn't hurting anyone. Okay, so I was only thirteen, but I wasn't hurting anyone!

The watchful eyes of neighbors and parents left my friends and me to occasionally play wiffle ball in the backyard or ride our bikes—that was it. How many times can you swing at a ball with holes in it? How often can you ride your bikes down the same streets and remain entertained?

I was thirteen years old, and yes, my friends and I smoked pot in the basement of my home. When friends entered the house, they would pass through the kitchen, visit briefly with my mom, grab a slice or two of fresh bread, dip it in Mom's soup, and shout hello to my dad, who would be seated in the den. Dad knew the names of every neighborhood kid. Our home was a place of safety, comfort, and familiarity. After getting their share of soup, they would make their way to the basement door. After opening it, they immediately walked into a lingering wall of marijuana aromatics.

Of course, my parents were aware of everything going on. You couldn't miss it. When you descended the stairs into the basement, the laundry room was on the left. We hung out on the right side of the room, where the Ping-Pong table, pool table, and Warp Warp video game were located. Some of the older guys, my brother's friends, would set a six-pack of beer outside the window before entering the house and then retrieve it once they were in the basement. I wasn't into drinking. It was much more convenient to take a hit. Mom and Dad reasoned that if we were going to smoke pot—and we were—they preferred we did it in the basement, under their supervision and where they knew we were safe. The basement was our sanctuary. It was a place where we could be ourselves without fear or judgment.

Back then, the pot wasn't that good. You had to smoke the whole fuckin' bag to get off! We usually had an inventory of Acapulco Gold, which was not too strong and not too weak. Occasionally, a seller would slip one of us some fool's gold. It was fake weed without a hint of cannabis. Ah, but then, there was hash. That was the real deal. You didn't mess with that stuff, but everybody smoked something. The best stuff was the Thai Sticks. Someone would get a bag of them and sell them for twenty-five dollars a stick.

Drugs were a pervasive presence on the streets of Monessen. Quaaludes and Parest were the most common. A lude could be bought for a dollar, and a few unscrupulous doctors would write prescriptions, or "scripts" as we called them, for fifteen dollars. Each script would yield thirty ludes, which could then be sold for five dollars each. They were more affordable and easier to obtain than a six-pack of beer. This drug culture was a significant part of our daily lives, influencing our decisions and actions.

Word quickly circulated when somebody got their hands on a script. We'd all meet at The Orbit, our local pool hall, and get whatever we wanted. Our friend's dad, August "Augie" Bucci, owned the pool hall. Mr. Bucci was a very well-respected businessman. The Orbit was also a meeting place for Mr. Bucci's numerous very well-dressed business associates—men who would arrive in black cars, wearing black suits. It did not go unnoticed, but it was never a topic of discussion.

Thanks to Miss Salotti, I made it through vocational school and advanced to seventh grade at Lincoln School, which was a transitional school meant to ease students into junior high school and later, high school. It was a one-year sentence, so I figured even I could make it through one year.

As it turned out, Lincoln was, by comparison, uneventful. I maintained my Ds and Fs, but I made it out and advanced to Monessen Junior High School for eighth grade. Although it was an eighth- and ninth-grade middle school, my dad was concerned about the quality of education and the influences I encountered. He transferred me to Mon Valley Catholic School to complete my ninth-grade.

Mon Valley Catholic School was a highly regarded, prestigious private school. I was, however, the only Jew in Mon Valley Catholic School—probably the only Jew ever to go there. It was ninth-grade, and I was fourteen years old. It was one full year of feeling out of place and the odd man out. The teachers, the administrators, and I all tried to make it work.

My dad got the call: "Mister Lieber, everyone at Mon Valley loves Bradley. He's a good boy." Dad waited for the inevitable but. "But Bradley just doesn't seem to want to go with the program."

I constantly struggled with my identity and the identities of everyone at Mon Valley. It wasn't that I didn't want to go with the program; I didn't understand the program! I didn't understand the titles they gave themselves. Take Father John, for instance. He was a nice guy, but he wasn't my father. I called him John. Sister Juanita and Sister Jean, same deal. I called them Juanita and Jean. I didn't mean any disrespect. They were very nice ladies, but not my sisters. There was no family resemblance whatsoever. What kind of family was I getting into, and who was I now, Brother Bradley? No, this was not my path, not my niche, not my religion, and not my family.

My parents and the administrators agreed it was best for me to leave the school. I was on a run; I'd made it through one year.

Dad's faith in me never wavered. He would confidently respond to anyone concerned that I just had to find my niche. He never told anyone. I wasn't even looking for it. I was looking for my next morsel of excitement, the next avenue of fun. I was beginning to determine what was important to me. Education was not on my list, but cars topped it. Cars were fun, fast, and exemplified success, and Pat Herron drove the hottest automobiles in town.

Pat lived across the street from my uncle and aunt. He was the eldest of two boys. His father, a doctor, passed away at a young age, leaving his mother, Ivy, to raise the boys. Ivy, a woman with a penchant for gambling, had a significant influence on her younger son, Rick, whom we'd nicknamed "Gook." I never would have imagined her influence on Gook would one day indirectly become an influence on me.

Pat was an inspirational figure to me. His cars—the 1962 candy apple red 427 Corvette split window and the candy apple red Chevelle 396—were my ultimate dream. I would watch in awe as Pat towed the Vette to the track with the Chevy. His cars symbolized success, and I often found myself standing on the curb, completely captivated by those two magnificent automobiles, thinking, "How the hell did he achieve this? Someday, I will, too!" His example became the driving force behind my aspirations, shaping my view of success and influencing my future decisions and actions.

My journey through education at Monessen High School was a tumultuous one. I was expected to complete my tenth, eleventh, and twelfth grades there, but my grades were not promising. I continued to get Ds and Fs, and I didn't care. Teachers would tell my parents the same story: "Bradley is a smart kid, but he doesn't apply himself." It was a constant battle, and I couldn't understand why my parents were putting themselves through it. The truth was, I didn't see the value in the education system. I didn't see how it could help me achieve my dreams, especially when I saw the struggles of the educated adults around me. This lack of faith in the system and the disillusionment with the adult world were significant challenges I faced throughout my adolescence.

Why should I care about something I didn't want to do? It seemed like a simple concept, and I had the grades to back myself up! But no one seemed to understand. The adults, the ones with the education, couldn't comprehend my perspective. They were the ones struggling, not me. With the changing economy and the slowing mills, what good did education do for the struggling employees and their employers? I was determined to find my path, regardless of their opinions. My determination to carve my own path, despite the odds, was unwavering.

My friends and I were products of our community. We never caused trouble, defaced property, or participated in delinquency; we just wanted to be together. Our community was like a well-rehearsed dance, with everyone doing their part day in and day out. It was so predictable and so routine. That's why so many of us turned to smoking pot to inject some much-needed excitement into our lives.

If we weren't in my basement or cruising the strip, we would hang out at Libby's Dairy Bar. We weren't hurting anybody, but like clockwork, the owner of Libby's would call the police. Like clockwork, Buckets would arrive. Buckets was our chief of police. I have no idea what his real name was. To everyone in the community, he was Buckets. He was a menacing dude, but God help him if he was ever involved in chasing someone on foot! There would be no chance. He'd be dead before making it half a block! Despite his intimidating appearance, Buckets was a familiar figure in our lives. He was the one who would heroically arrive to save the Dairy Bar from our loitering, and we would escape his capture only to repeat the same thing on another day. I'd just run across the street to my aunt and uncle's house. I'd run inside, and my aunt would casually say, "The police are on their way, aren't they?" It was all part of life in Monessen.

Despite my accumulating history of academic struggles, my parents decided to give Monessen High School a shot for the tenth, eleventh, and twelfth grades. The road was far from smooth. I barely scraped through the tenth grade and made it to the eleventh. To my surprise, I excelled in the eleventh grade, so much so that the school authorities suggested I repeat that year!

The thought of returning to Monessen High School to repeat my failed eleventh year was untenable. Unbeknownst to me, my parents recognized that continual rejection and repeated failures were causing me to become more reckless with my life. That was all about to change.

A script had been written, and distribution of quaaludes was occurring at The Orbit. Bobby Span, a friend, had a couple and was willing to share. He gave me one and told me to take it. The plan was that he would follow me home, I would park the car in the driveway, and then we would go cruising together. It sounded cool to me, so I popped the lude.

By the time I reached my parents' house, I was in a terrible state. I forgot to step on the brake and drove my dad's car into the garage door. Dad emerged from the house, more furious than I'd ever seen him. Behind me, Bobby beeped the horn, waved, and continued on his way without me. This incident was a turning point for my dad. It made him realize the dangerous path I was on and the urgent need for change.

Chapter 3
Grand River Academy

G rand River Academy was more than just a school. It was a community where I never felt abandoned or punished. My parents had already instilled in me a strong foundation of love and confidence. I never doubted their intentions. Grand River was another adventure, another opportunity to meet new friends. It became a place where I felt understood and could understand others, a community where the other parents were like mine. I felt I truly belonged for the first time since my experience in the Cub Scouts, Den 510.

Grand River Academy was not your typical all-boys school. We were not delinquent boys but boys who did not fit society's mold. The students were bright, but we were frustrated with the often overbearing and condescending instructors in conventional schools. Grand River didn't force us to conform to an arbitrary image for unexplained reasons. Instead, it focused on our individual stories and reasons for being there, a unique approach that intrigued and benefited each of us. It was a place where one felt seen and understood. You were not just another student in the crowd.

Don't get me wrong; the teachers were people with authority. If you stepped over the line, you experienced their punishment. But for the most part, they became friends. The teachers treated each of us as equals. They required respect but were willing to offer respect freely in return. Teachers knew that every student was there for a reason. Each student had his or her own story.

The teachers and students were on a first-name basis. Take, for instance, Mr. Menzee. We all knew him as Zeek. Tim Burke was called Tim unless other adults were around. When they were, we showed our respect by calling him Mr. Burke. It was awkward, though, because Tim was one of those special teachers who had become a close personal friend. Then there was the basketball coach, Joe Camelli, who was the exception. We called him Mr. Camelli or Coach. He was a big dude. It wasn't quite the same with him, but he still treated us with respect!

Academically, I still wasn't an all-star student, but I did settle down a little. It was the respect I received from my teachers that prompted my improvement. They'd assigned Mike Buck as my roommate. Mike attended Grand River Academy with his two brothers, Jeff and Rob. He was a hard-ass wrestler. The administration figured an impression would be made by assigning us to a room together in West Hall, our dorm. They were right; I almost ruined him!

I discovered I was even worse at basketball than academics, but Coach Camelli needed a sixth body on the team. I don't even know what position I played. I just ran around the court, cheering my team-mates on. Occasionally, someone would accidentally throw me the ball. I'd quickly find someone to throw it back to. It wasn't much of a game to me. Be present, stay out of the way, run up and down the court, and avoid getting a pass. Those were my instructions.

So, did Grand River Academy's newfound acceptance impact my desire to have fun? Not really. Basketball was fun, but not as much fun as smoking pot. This transition from feeling accepted to engaging in risky behavior was a personal choice, not a reflection of the school's influence.

At sixteen, I'd become quite the entrepreneur. Someone would purchase a pound of pot. I would buy a quarter pound from him, sell three ounces, and keep one ounce. The sale of the three ounces would cover the cost of my one ounce—and they thought I wasn't learning.

I attended Grand River Academy from 1970 through 1971. Although I wasn't an all-star student, I did better than in my previous academic experiences. I almost made it through my first year. Mr. Curry, Richard, an English teacher, caught me smoking pot in the dorm. Was I the only one? No, I was the only one who didn't escape through my dorm window in time. One month before finishing my eleventh grade, I was again booted out of school.

Over the summer, Mr. Curry contacted my dad and told him the administration realized I wasn't a bad kid; it was a single infraction, a mistake. He believed I'd learned from it. He said he thought there was hope for me and wanted to invite me back for my last year. I did learn my lesson. I knew never to smoke pot in my dorm without keeping an ear out for anyone coming down the hall! Unfortunately, Ron Ross, my dorm master, wore soft-sole shoes. To this day, I hold the distinction of being the only boy kicked out of Grand River Academy twice for the same reason!

I'd blown my chance to complete my education at Grand River. Did I care? Not really. I missed some guys, but Grand River was one of many in my repetitive educational experiences. I was not meant for school. I didn't work hard for something I didn't want. I couldn't take something seriously that made no sense to me. Dad sent my brother, Steve, to pick me up and take me to Painesville, Ohio, to live with him for a few months. Like me and everyone else, Steve was not foreign to the drug culture of the 1960s and 1970s. Some might have thought I was jumping from the pot into the fire, but my dad reasoned that with Steve, at least it was a controlled burn.

My elder brothers, Steve and Bob, played significant roles in my life. They were there; they showed up. At times, they showed up when I didn't want them to. Nevertheless, they were there for me. Their presence, actions, and guidance, whether I appreciated it at the time or not, shaped my understanding of family and responsibility.

When I was sixteen, I went to the local bar with friends. I looked older, or maybe the bartender had low sales that day. He was willing to serve us until my brother Bob entered the bar.

"See that kid? That's my brother. He's sixteen! Get him the fuck outta here, and I don't ever want to catch you serving him again!" Bob was direct and unwavering in projecting what might happen to the bartender if I was allowed to enter again. I didn't like it then, but Bob was teaching me values.

Steve and Bob were twins, six years my senior, but no two people could be more different. Bob worked in the steel mills, a quintessential product of Monessen. When the mills closed, it was a difficult adjustment for him. For a time, he moved to California with Janet and me. Later, he moved to Arizona to live with my cousins. Bob ultimately became a security guard, which was the perfect job for him. He loved people and loved to talk with them. He spoke to everyone, whether they wanted to talk or not. They would be walking away, and Bob would be smiling ear-to-ear, still talking, oblivious that they were fading into the distance.

Bob was dyslexic before anyone knew such a thing existed. Yet, Bob loved to read. Later, when Janet and I lived in Marina Del Rey, Bob would call me weekly to see how I was doing and talk about whatever book he was reading. By the end of the conversation, I knew the plot, the characters, and the synopsis. Bob's enjoyment of people and his concern for me and my well-being tremendously impacted my awareness of those I encountered. Many years later, I would honor Bob at the Monessen Public Library with a donation in his name. The Monessen Public Library dedicated the Reading Room to Bob's memory. There, a plaque honoring his name will forever remain.

Steve, on the other hand, was never a passive participant. Steve was a mover and shaker. He was a member of the American Federation of State, County, and Municipal Employees (AFSCME) and became a union representative, a position he held for thirty years. He was selected as a state delegate for the election of President Barack Obama. Steve also taught me values, but in a different way. Steve taught me the value of treating others fairly. His impact went further than the individuals surrounding him. He recognized that his decisions could impact hundreds of people he may never meet. Steve taught me perspective, looking beyond the present and remembering that the decisions I make today will affect my future and, potentially, the future of others. His lessons on fairness and perspective have shaped my approach to life and decision-making.

So, there I was in Painesville, Ohio, with my brother Steve. I was directionless, uneducated, and jobless. Steve, understanding the importance of education, was determined to change that. Hell, in my mind, I had been doing nothing but learning, but he had a different plan.

He enrolled me at Painesville's local high school. I was there for such a short time that I can't remember the school's name. One of Steve's coworkers, Sandra Mapes, had a badass 440 Dodge Charger. She was a nice gal, and she let me drive her car to school, thinking it would help me fit in with the other kids. It was a nice gesture, and I appreciated it. There was one small problem: everyone thought I was a narc. They avoided me like the plague! My education there lasted about a month.

Since the new high school didn't work out, Steve turned to Plan B: getting Bradley a job.

He explained to me that I would have to work my way up. I couldn't expect to start at the top of any business. Truer words were never spoken. He got me a job at the local nursing home. I started at the bottom: I was assigned to clean the bedpans! I told the supervisor, "I am outta here!" She begged me to stay and reassigned me to work with the nursing home janitor, Davey Jones. It wasn't a bad job. I stayed with them for another week.

Steve would not give up on getting me a job, though I secretly wished he would. He got me a job at Charlie's Hamburgers, flipping burgers and counting other people's money. Nope, that was not going to happen. That was another endeavor that lasted only a couple of weeks.

At that point, Steve saw I was not adapting to his suggestions. He must have discussed the situation with our parents, but if he did, he never told me about it. He enrolled me at Tusculum University in Tennessee.

You would have thought these well-meaning individuals in my life might have begun to see a pattern forming by now and dropped the idea of schooling.

The quote, "Insanity is doing the same thing over and over again and expecting different results," is usually attributed to Albert Einstein. I'd proven the statement true, whether it was something Einstein said or not. Once again, I was enrolled in a school for students who didn't fit into the big college and university programs. It was a small school, not necessarily memorable. I became friends with Ramone and Gustavo, two fellas from Peru. These were the two best-looking guys I'd ever seen, and they came from a lot of money. I knew they had family money because they ran up bar tabs all over town until their families would send them five to ten thousand dollars, and they would go around to each bar and pay off their debts.

The two didn't live on campus. They lived in a two- or three-bedroom trailer tucked away in the beautiful Smoky Mountains. I'd never experienced a paradise like that. The low-hanging fog framed jutting yellow birch trees, buckeyes, and magnolias. There were a variety of shrubs and vines at its base. The backdrop was a wall of jagged rock. And in the middle of all this beauty was Ramone and Gustavo's trailer. I spent a lot of my time with them. Although I'd moved around to numerous places, at Ramone and Gustavo's place, I finally felt the satisfaction of being on my own.

The two of them were not at Tusculum for an education. They'd mentioned that their country was undergoing political upheaval, and their parents wanted them safe in the United States. Nothing could be safer than Tusculum. It was in a perpetual time warp of boredom. I lasted six months. Ramone and Gustavo were not there much longer than I was.

After Tusculum didn't work, Steve sent me to Kent State University, his alma mater. It had been good for Steve, but I hated it.

Here's the thing. Anyone could rightly judge me for failing in school. As I've mentioned several times, I didn't like school. But one thing became very obvious to me: all those who might judge me—those who had an education, went on to college, remained in Monessen—

were unhappy. Having completed their education, all of them were looking for jobs, just like me. Teachers were looking for jobs, just like me. Steel mill supervisors were looking for jobs, just like me. What had their educations provided for them that set them apart from me? Nothing!

I finished a year at Kent State University, which, based on my track record, was good enough. I wanted to make some money!

I decided to return to Monessen to figure out my next move. Before returning, I stopped at the Oldsmobile dealership in Greensburg, Pennsylvania, and paid $7,800 cash for a new 1988 Oldsmobile. It was as black as midnight, interior and exterior, with a moonroof accentuating its beauty. In Monessen, everyone wondered how the hell I was driving a new car when I hadn't finished school and had no job. They knew my parents didn't buy it for me.

My dad pulled me aside and asked how I was driving a new car. I might not have had an education that met the neighborhood's standards, and I might not have followed the community's path of working in the mills. But I knew how to sell and how to save. I bought the Oldsmobile selling pot.

I thought he would have been prouder. He didn't lecture me or even bat an eye, but simply said, "Bradley, you need to have a job. People are going to start talking," which only meant that people were already talking.

Dad called Eric Percheski, a neighbor who lived across the street. Eric owned a junkyard and was happy to offer me a job I wasn't looking for. I don't know what I'd ever done to him, but he put me on the shittiest job he could find. He had me change the filters on his massive steel crushing machines. I was covered from head to toe in oil and grease. Three weeks of slime, and I said, "Fuck this. I'd rather be in school!"

Patient and understanding, my dad kept telling himself and anyone who asked, "Bradley simply has to find his niche." So, I bummed around a bit, you know, looking for my niche. My lack of enthusiasm for finding a job encouraged my dad to, once again, find one for me.

"Bradley, I've got you an interview with Mr. Frank Wentz, the store manager at Wickes Furniture Store."

If my dad had ever found himself looking for a job, he would have done well starting an employment agency. He was not just a father but also a mentor who believed in me. He was a successful salesman who saw in me the potential to become anything I wanted to be, and he was focused on my natural ability to sell. He believed that if he could introduce me to the right opportunity under the watchful eye of someone other than himself, I would rise to the occasion.

"I think he might have a job for you," Dad said.

I tried to explain to my dad that I wasn't looking for a job; I was looking for my niche. I was a good salesman, but not good enough to convince my dad that I was making any effort to find that elusive niche. Dad wasn't buying that one.

"I want you to call him and set up that interview." The tone in my dad's voice told me this was not a suggestion but an ultimatum.

I gave Mr. Wentz a call. His South Carolinian accent conveyed a magnetic friendliness that eased my mind about seeing him. I was not expecting the massive human being that greeted me when I arrived. Frank was at least six-foot-three with an enormous pair of hands that engulfed mine when we greeted each other with a handshake. Our interview was more like two salesmen sharing war stories; we hit it off well.

After interviewing with Frank, I was hired as a furniture salesman. Selling furniture was easy for me, and I knew I could make $35K if I applied myself. I loved helping people, being appreciated, and, most of all, making money. I took advantage of the spiffs Wickes gave out for selling mattresses. If you sold a king-size Beautyrest mattress and box spring, you received an additional fifty bucks for the sale. It was in addition to any commissions—a bonus! The way I saw it, I was being handed an extra fifty bucks for what I was doing, anyway. I sold the hell out of those mattresses. However, it didn't take a college degree to foresee that selling furniture in an area dependent on the steel mills that were rapidly shutting down would not be a long-term place of employment.

I liked Frank. I could tell that he wanted more out of life and would do whatever it took to get it. It wasn't long before Frank moved to San Diego, California, to do exactly what I wanted: get out of Pennsylvania and live life to the fullest.

Before leaving, Frank told me he'd pave the way for me in California if I ever considered moving. California; I just chuckled.

Chapter 4
Dutch's Invitations

I t was sadly obvious that Monessen was dying. What had been a thriving community was becoming a ghost town. Windows were boarded on Main Street, and homes were facing foreclosure. The exodus of families dependent on paychecks from the steel mills and associated auxiliary fabrication was irreversible.

My buddy Danny "Dutch" Gladys and Cindy, still his girlfriend, had completed their college educations. He received his degree from Dickinson College, a private college in Pennsylvania, and she received hers from Indiana University. They'd returned to Monessen, and Aetna Insurance immediately hired Cindy.

Cindy's education worked for her. She did well in the insurance industry, and Aetna Insurance soon transferred her to Southern California. Dutch was up for new experiences, so they moved to Yorba Linda, California. On Friday nights they would go to happy hour, get a slight buzz on, and give me a call, extolling the virtues of living in Southern California and encouraging me to pull up stakes and make a move. At the end of the calls, I would offer a noncommittal chuckle at the suggestion.

"Dutch, I'll tell you what," I finally said during one of the calls.

"Why don't I come out there and visit you two? I'll save you the dime for the Friday night telephone calls."

"What's stopping you?" Dutch replied.

After that conversation, I made my first visit to California. Dutch and Cindy met me at John Wayne Airport in Orange County.

Dutch was exuberant. "Man, it's great to see you! I didn't think you'd really come. Wait until you see this place. I'm telling you, Brad, you will not believe it!"

Driving down the Pacific Coast Highway from Newport to Laguna and gazing at the houses overlooking the ocean, I was in awe.

Dutch leaned forward, pointing upward through the windshield. "You see those houses up there on the cliff?" His voice was filled with admiration. He paused, allowing me to continue admiring the massive structures. "Each of them costs at least $150,000!"

My jaw dropped. "Wow! How could they ever afford that?"

A sudden surge went through me. It was a feeling I remembered experiencing as a kid every time Pat Herron passed by in his candy apple red Chevy 396, towing his 1962 427 split window candy apple red Corvette.

That vision of Pat remained in my mind as we continued driving. I realized that the allure of California was not just in its scenic beauty but in the opportunities it offered. It didn't matter how the people who lived in those houses on the cliff managed to succeed; the important thing was that they did! If they could achieve it, so could I. All I had to do was work hard and be smart about it. Without even being aware of it, I was quietly considering the possibility. Could California be my next move?

My five-day visit was a much-needed escape from the daily repetition of my life in Monessen. It was a time of exploration and reminiscing about our shared past. Cindy's culinary skills kept us all well-fed and content. It was a relief to leave behind the despair of a dying city. Southern California was a breath of fresh air, a stark contrast to what was rapidly becoming known as "The Rust Belt" of Pennsylvania.

The energy, the opportunities, and the natural beauty were a world away from the desolation and stagnation of Monessen.

As my departure from California approached, I couldn't shake off a sense of melancholy. It wasn't so much about leaving California, but about bidding farewell to two friends who had been a constant source of inspiration and support. After I left, their success was not just a memory, but a driving force that would continue to motivate me.

Back in Monessen, the days became weeks, and the weeks became months. It didn't make much difference what day it was; they were all the same. Even Buckets had left, and a new police captain was adjusting to the rigors of locating lost pets, returning grocery carts, and responding to the emergency calls of lonely widows in the valley. Occasionally, there would be some action, like when delinquents would spray-paint boarded buildings, but the city was dying. Even Libby's Dairy Bar longed for the days when our cars filled its parking lot. The feeling of being left behind in a dying town was like a weight on my shoulders, a constant reminder of the need for change.

Everybody was getting the itch to move on. Rick Herron, "Gook," and a buddy of his made a similar trip to mine. Theirs was a road trip to Las Vegas and California. However, when it was time for them to return, Gook surprised his friend by telling him, "You'll need to get a plane ticket home because I'm not going back." And he didn't.

Rick Herron, undoubtedly inspired by his mother Ivy, became one of Las Vegas, Nevada's most successful and influential linemakers. He was the original. Rick started as a ticket writer at the Barbary Coast, working for Jimmy Vacarro. He became the Sports Book Manager at the Fremont and then the Race and Sports Book Director at the Sands. He then became the Race and Sports Book Manager at the Las Vegas Hilton SuperBook.

And the Friday evening calls from Dutch and Cindy continued, reminding me of my misery. It wasn't a single call that finally shook me into reality. It may have been the accumulation of all of them. Eventually, those calls had to end.

"Hey Brad, it's Dutch," Danny yelled.

"I know who it is. Where are you?" As if I didn't know.

"Hey! It's Friday. We're at happy hour. There's only one thing missing."

"Yeah, what's that?" I asked.

"You, Brad, listen to me. You've got to make a move. Cindy and I are hoping you can come to California. It's where it's happening! You saw it for yourself! Look, you can stay with us until you get settled. We've already talked about it." Their unwavering support and belief in me were like a beacon of hope in the fog of uncertainty.

I responded, "Oh, it's tempting, but I don't know. It's a big move."

"Brad, you could be here by New Year's Eve! Let's celebrate it together! We'll welcome 1980 like old times!"

That was my last Friday night call from Dutch and Cindy.

Harrriet and Herschel Lieber

The alley entrance to Dad's and Uncle
Jerry's furniture store
Photo Courtesy of Donora Historical Society

L to R: Mom, Grandma Gertrude, Great
Grandma Rose Herskowitz

Our home at 40 Colonial Drive

Grand River Academy

My reunion with Mrs. Salotti

Waiting for "Buckets" to arrive

Chapter 5
California, Here I Come!

W hat the hell? I couldn't keep turning down Dutch and Cindy; they were my friends! I wasn't sure if moving to California was right, but I knew I had to try.

On December 20, 1979, at ten o'clock in the morning, the weather was a balmy thirty-one degrees Fahrenheit, with winds blowing at five miles per hour from the south. With one thousand dollars in my pocket —a significant amount for a young person at the time—I left Monessen, Pennsylvania, and Wickes Furniture Store for good. My mission there was complete. I knew a good percentage of the population in Monessen was sleeping comfortably because of the number of Beautyrest mattresses I'd sold.

By then, I'd also sold the Oldsmobile and bought a sleek, silver Mazda RX7 with a sunroof. I'd taken it out on a $277 monthly payment. I didn't know how I would make the payments, but somehow, I always did. I loved that car. I loved the lines, the color, and the speed.

The cross-country drive felt like a blur. I was on a mission, not a sightseeing tour. Along the way, I made a few brief stops to visit friends who had also left Pennsylvania. Their stories and support were invaluable to me as I took this leap. I needed to keep moving, but their encouragement stayed with me. It didn't matter if I made it to California or only halfway; there was no turning back!

On December 31, 1979, at around five o'clock in the afternoon, I pulled my Mazda RX-7, filled with all my earthly possessions, behind Dutch and Cindy's condominium garage—and they were waiting for me. A sudden rush of accomplishment enveloped me. I had done it. I had taken the first significant step of personal responsibility in building my new life.

No one had sent me to California or paved my way. Until that moment, I'd felt lost in life. I wasn't unhappy—I was the happiest person I knew—but I felt aimless. Dad always made excuses for me by saying I was looking for my niche. That wasn't necessarily correct. I was searching for my destination. I figured that if I could pinpoint a destination, I could figure out a niche to get me there.

I remember thinking, "All I have to do is make $35,000 a year, and I'm golden!" I would own my life and never have to go back.

The $28,000 a year I had earned from Wickes Furniture would be a great starting point. But then I recalled the $150,000 homes along the Pacific Coast Highway I had seen during my previous visit. Instantly, the $1,000 in my pocket and my last $28,000 salary seemed insignificant in this new world of flashy cars and Rolexes. But I was not deterred. I was optimistic and determined. I had made it to California, and I was about to begin a new and exciting journey filled with possibilities.

It was a significant turning point in my life. Although I still didn't have a specific destination, I was determined to keep looking for it and pursuing it, convinced it was just around the next corner. I believed that if I kept moving forward, taking risks, investing time, and showing up, I would ultimately find my destination, establish the means to reach it, and fulfill my destiny.

Witnessing others' successes inspired me to realize that life can be whatever you want it to be—all you have to do is earn it. I'd heard that the road to success is paved in gold, but I was now beginning to realize that I had to get on my hands and knees and be the one to pave it. The transformative power of hard work was within my reach!

We unloaded all of my belongings from the Mazda and proceeded to Dutch and Cindy's condo. Unfortunately, it only took one trip to empty the car, but that was okay with me. It was all going to change.

I was greeted by Midas, Dutch and Cindy's golden retriever. I took Midas's name as another positive omen.

I felt ready to hit the ground running. I couldn't wait to start the new job set up for me by my former manager, Frank Wentz. Little did I know, things were about to take an unexpected turn.

"I'm sorry, sir, but Mr. Wentz is no longer employed at Wickes Furniture," the voice on the other end of the phone said in comforting tones, almost as if delivering news of his passing to an unsuspecting family member.

The news hit me like a ton of bricks. "What do you mean, 'he is no longer employed at Wickes?'" I asked, my voice trembling with disbelief.

"Sir, he was only here briefly before finding employment elsewhere. He is no longer with Wickes."

"Well, I'm sure he left my name," I insisted. "I need to speak to whomever he talked to, whoever is hiring."

"What did you say your name is?" the gentleman asked.

"Bradley Lieber, but you can call me Brad," I replied. "I'm from Monessen, Pennsylvania. I worked for Frank in Pittsburgh. He must have mentioned me to someone. I was supposed to have a job when I got out here."

"Well, Mr. Lieber, I'm sorry. I've never heard of you. Mr. Wentz never mentioned you to me, and I am the manager of Wickes Furniture. I am the one who does the hiring, and I currently have no openings."

I hung up the telephone in disbelief and explained my situation to Dutch.

"What am I going to do?" I pondered, my mind a whirlwind of uncertainty. I wasn't seeking a definitive answer as much as I was trying to navigate the maze of my options.

Dutch's intensity was palpable. He seized on my question and, without hesitation, declared, "You'll get a job."

Well, hell, I knew that, but Dutch persisted before I could even gather my thoughts. "You'll get a job at the Levitz furniture store."

Chapter 6
You'll Love It at Levitz

Interviewing, often perceived as daunting, was surprisingly effortless for me. A wave of calm and confidence washed over me as I entered the room. "If this role is a good fit for me, great! If not, then it's not the place for me," I thought, embracing my authenticity.

When I showed up to meet Tom, there was an immediate spark, an electric connection, whether it stemmed from his keen eye for talent or perhaps my natural charisma and humility.

"Can you sell?" he asked, his gaze piercing.

I flashed him a confident smile, determined to make an impression. "What exactly are you looking for, and how can I help you get there?" I responded, ready to turn this into an opportunity.

I started a week later.

Levitz wasn't selling the high-end furniture that filled my childhood home—nothing like what my dad and uncle sold. Levitz Furniture was practical and accessible. The majority of our clientele were renters dipping their toes into adulthood. There were only a handful of first-time home owners to break the monotony. The reality was that Levitz furniture often had a shorter lifespan than the leases of the clients' apartments.

Speaking of apartments, since I now had a job, it was time to move out of Dutch and Cindy's place. I found an apartment in Huntington Beach. There was one drawback: I didn't have the $360 a month for rent. I knew that unless the manager allowed me to pay half of the rent twice a month, other things would come up, and I would never have the whole amount at the beginning of the month. So, I asked the manager if I could pay $180 every two weeks. He appreciated my honesty.

"You know what? Since you told me about your situation upfront, I will let you do that. You pay me $180 every two weeks. That should help you budget."

For a potential customer, walking into a Levitz store was like navigating a gauntlet. As they entered, salespeople flanked both sides of the entrance, each poised to pounce with their rehearsed pitches. My approach, however, was refreshingly different. I welcomed customers with a warm smile, ready to engage as a friend rather than a sales predator. I wasn't there to trap them but to build connections, which paid off handsomely.

It didn't take long for my unique style to catch the attention of the other salespeople. They began to realize that I wasn't just another face in the crowd—I was a force to be reckoned with. As I continued to rack up results and my methods became transparent, inspiring others while setting myself apart. My hard work culminated in a beautiful gold ring adorned with stunning diamonds, a mark of my achievement: the Levitz President's Club Award. More than the accolade, what truly mattered was that I had unearthed my true self through this journey.

I gave my buddy Gook a call to see how he was doing in Las Vegas.

"Bradley, just come visit!" he said. "We're not that far from each other."

From my lack of an enthusiastic response, he could sense that a vacation in Las Vegas was not in my budget. I didn't have money for food, but I had enough to get there and back.

"Bradley, I'll give you passes for food in the buffet line!"

This inspired a more positive response. "Fuck, I'm in!"

Seeing Gook's success, and experiencing a measure of success myself at Levitz, crystallized a realization: I had stumbled upon my calling, a niche I had unknowingly inhabited all my life. I was destined for sales. My lineage was rich with entrepreneurs—grandparents, parents, uncles—and salesmanship had been woven through the fabric of my family. Even the guys selling weed at the pool hall were in the game! It turned out that I didn't need to search far and wide for my niche. I'd been in it all along. I just needed to discover—WHO I WAS.

Not long after that, whether it was a matter of competitive survival or authentic encouragement, some of the older salespeople approached me.

"Brad, you've got to get out of here. You need to get into outside sales—that's where the money is."

Their words haunted me. I knew who I was, and I knew I could sell. I needed only to find the right vehicle to make the kind of real money that could buy my independence. Perhaps it was on the outside.

Chapter 7
Working on the Outside

The ad stated that Copy R, a Minolta dealership, was looking for a copier salesperson.

I called the telephone number listed and scheduled an interview with Kerry. I told him I wanted to sell copiers. He didn't spend much time on the telephone with me. If first impressions were to be considered, from our brief telephone conversation, I thought him a bit brash, even rude. Nevertheless, I showed up.

Kerry was, as I had expected, rude as hell. I was taken aback by the abruptness of his first words in the interview: "So, you want to sell copiers, huh?"

I flashed him my overpowering Lieber smile and said, "Yes, I'm your man."

The smile didn't faze him at all. He remained expressionless.

"Where you gonna put 'em?" he asked, eyeing my prized possession, my Mazda RX7, with disgust.

His words left me speechless, unsure of how to react, but Kerry was not done.

"If you want to sell copiers, come back here with a station wagon, and I'll hire you to sell copiers."

So, I ended my first interview with Kerry and the relationship I'd enjoyed with my Mazda RX7. I immediately traded it for a gold Toyota Corolla Wagon and drove back to Copy R.

This time, there would be no interview, no discussion. I had no questions about the outcome of this visit. I approached Kerry, and before he could say a word, I told him, "I'm selling your copiers now because I have a station wagon. I got rid of the car I loved and traded it in for a lousy station wagon. When do I start?"

I started immediately.

Copiers were the new thing. You were considered high-tech if you could make legible copies without using a ditto machine. I would load a copier onto a gurney, shove it into the back of my Toyota wagon, and drive around demonstrating it to anyone who would stop and listen. Hell, the copier was on a gurney—I'd follow people if they didn't stop!

Dutch got a kick out of the old Toyota. Occasionally, we'd meet for drinks on a Friday evening at some swanky joint. Cars were a big deal back then, a sign of status and success. The parking lot looked like a shot from Lifestyles of the Rich and Famous, and there I was, pulling in with my gold Toyota station wagon.

If anyone at the bar ever asked me what kind of car I was driving, and they did, I would tell them, "I'm driving a Gold Arrow." No one ever questioned me, so I left the vision of a little-known, expensive European automobile lingering in their minds.

Early in my new career, I had a revelation. I didn't need to be the best at everything. I just had to understand the business, master what I needed to know, and be exceptional at the specific thing I was doing. This realization was liberating, empowering me to focus on my strengths and excel in my role.

Copy R was not the place for an energetic fella. I'd found the right vehicle for my success—sales. Unfortunately, I wasn't driving the right vehicle for my vision. Still behind the wheel of that old gold Toyota station wagon, I had visions of being behind the wheel of my first candy-apple red Ferrari! But I wouldn't get there with the $1,200 monthly for three months plus commissions Copy R was offering. It was their make-or-break deal. I soon realized what they were saying. Make it and stay broke!

Bill Kelly was a coworker of mine. We'd been on several sales calls and deliveries together, and he'd been observing me.

"Brad, let's face it," he said. "You'll never get to where you want to go working at Copy R. I want you to meet my former employer."

My first thought was, "If your former employer was so great, why are you working at Copy R?" But Bill immediately caught my confusion. Without going into all the details, he explained that he'd made a costly mistake for which he took full responsibility. While he still held Monroe Systems in high regard and greatly appreciated his former boss, he'd forfeited an opportunity to return. Bill was nice enough to contact his former boss and tell him that the two of us should meet.

Monroe Systems distributed various copiers, calculators, and accounting machines. Working for them would broaden my product line and increase my opportunities to make money. So, Bill paved the way for me to meet his former boss, Bernie Huot, the manager of Monroe Systems. I called, and he told me he knew of me and was expecting to hear from me.

Bernie Huot was tremendously influential in my life. He was unusual. He appeared to genuinely want his employees to be happy. He was interested in my goals and how Monroe Systems would assist me in achieving them. This made a powerful impression on me. I felt very comfortable with Bernie, and the feeling was mutual. He'd heard about my ability to sell and hired me to be his copier sales manager. The move surprised me, so I asked him why he'd done it.

"You're not a sales manager," he sternly replied. "I hired you because you can sell more than anyone. You're not a sales manager until I see people coming to you with questions and you responding to them with the correct answers." He paused for a moment to let that statement sink in. "Brad, you need to lead people. You need to take them to places they could not go on their own. When you can do that, then you're the manager."

It was an important lesson. I could manage my direction, initiative, purpose, and work ethic, but could I positively influence those reporting to me? Caring for and managing people would be the difference between having and growing a business.

"The first thing we've got to do is get you a place to live," he said. "You've got to get out of that apartment. Here's what we're gonna do. There's a group of condominiums here in Huntington Beach. We'll split it fifty-fifty. You make the $600 mortgage payments; I'll put up the deposit. It will give you a chance to establish some equity."

Bernie's approach was unique. He had done this with other employees, and no strings were attached. The arrangement was as simple as he'd presented. He profited by locking his good employees in, while his employees profited from the opportunity to build equity. It was an extension of his care for his employees. There were no games with Bernie. Any one of us could have bought him out of a condo at any given time.

He was also predictable. His message was the same to every employee. "You want to see me? I'm here every morning at five o'clock, having my coffee. You want to have coffee with me? Be here at five o'clock, and we'll have coffee and talk." After eight o'clock, we never saw him.

There was something very special about this man. I wanted to learn from him, so I showed up at five o'clock at least three times a week. It wasn't so much to spend time with him; it was to invest time with him. This was one of the essential lessons I learned from Bernie. He was a tremendous example of time management. And he was fair to his employees. If one of them preferred to finish their sleep, get to work on time, and do a good job, Bernie appreciated it. However, if employees were not investing in themselves, he had little reason to invest in them with additional time and wisdom.

Bernie had expectations and demands. If an employee did not meet them, they were gone and forgotten. He increased his expectations for anyone who was particularly ambitious and rewarded the employees' achievements as if they were heroes. His high expectations created an insatiable determination in us to meet and exceed them. He made me want to succeed, and his influence flowed into every aspect of life.

At Monroe Systems, I wasn't just learning; I was thriving. Bernie's guidance, my relentless effort, and my unwavering enthusiasm were the key ingredients in my success. His influence didn't just teach me the art of attracting an audience; it empowered me to sell copiers like there was no tomorrow. I would stay in a potential client's office until they made a purchase, and when technology advanced to allow image resizing, I was golden!

My approach was anything but conventional, and that's what led to my success. When I took my copier to a hospital or a doctor's office, the potential customer expected me to be like any other salesperson and just drop the copier off. But that wasn't my style. When I walked in, that copier was still mine. It was a valuable piece of technology for which I was responsible. It was only logical and appropriate for the product expert—me—to explain its functions to the person evaluating it.

I believed that my product had the power to enhance the lives of everyone I met. I couldn't bear to leave an office without giving potential customers a taste of its benefits. It wouldn't have been right for me to do so. I was driven by the deep-seated belief that I was making a positive difference in their lives.

Transcending the role of a salesperson, I became a performer on their stage, captivating everyone who witnessed my magic! As I navigated their offices, hallways, and production plants, I became the topic of discussion at the water cooler. My engagement with each customer left a lasting impression as I made sure they felt involved and connected at every step of the process.

My technique was no secret. I took pleasure in making friends, winning people over, and making them eager to do business with me. While they were confined to their offices, I was out there, having a blast in the world. My presence became a welcome respite from their daily stress. And if I had what they needed, there was no reason for them to look elsewhere. Why would they?

I created lasting relationships by prioritizing my customers' needs and ensuring their ongoing support. I never needed to sell them again. My dedication to service made them customers for life. I made it easy for them to acquire what they needed. They decided to purchase from me before they saw what I had to offer because they were investing in me and my commitment to eliminate any challenges that might otherwise interrupt their business. I was an available friend who made it a point to know my business, their business, and what they needed to be successful.

Bernie was also a man with common sense. I recall a copier Al Curry, a sales associate of mine, sold to a company in Compton, California. He'd sold them an RL612 beauty. It had all the bells and whistles on it. He sold it, the service guys delivered it and set it up, and Al and I went to the site to show the buyer all of its features and proper care.

When we arrived at the facility, Al approached the individual he'd sold the copier to and said, "Hey, man. How are you doing? I'm here to show you how to use your copier."

The guy looked at him and said, "I've never seen you before in my life."

At first, it confused me. I interjected, "Hey, we just sold you the copier the other day. You signed for it and everything. We have proof of delivery and—"

He interrupted me. It was a substantial interruption that was more of a warning than a response. "I have no idea who you are. I've never seen you before in my life!"

I motioned to Al, and we made our way back to the car. It was obvious. The copier went in the front door and out the back. Wherever the copier was now, this guy was never going to admit he'd ordered it. We'd been had. When we returned to the office, we apologetically explained the situation to Bernie, knowing that with his wisdom, he would know of a way to turn the tables on this thief. He smiled knowingly, and his advice was not only wise; it was based on common sense.

"Fellas, let's just leave him alone. Don't worry about the copier." He paused and concluded, "It isn't worth getting shot."

I depended a great deal on Bernie. His inspiration not only influenced my work performance but also my life. For anyone willing to invest a few five o'clock mornings, he offered young, impetuous dreamers like me the tools to become mature and confident men.

Unfortunately for me, Monroe Systems' engine, Bernie Huot, announced his departure from the company just as things were beginning to progress for me. It's remarkable how one person's inspiration, energy, and encouragement can shape a team's success. With his exit, a new manager named Frank took over. Unfortunately, Frank's leadership style was in stark contrast to Bernie's, which significantly affected the team's dynamics. Everything Bernie was, Frank was not. He was a prick!

Once again, I found myself discussing my career situation with Dutch. His immediate response was both simple and profound: "Contact a headhunter. Seize the opportunity." His straightforward advice made me realize this was an opportunity. I'd already accumulated several success stories in the office and business machines industry. After leaving Levitz, Copy R, and now Monroe Systems on good terms, I knew I would be an asset to any company willing to hire me.

So, I reached out to a headhunter, and it wasn't long before I received a call. They informed me that someone was interested in talking to me, which was encouraging since I realized my days at Monroe were numbered. We scheduled an interview at the headhunter's office for the following Monday. When I asked what the company did, I learned they sold furniture. A sinking feeling washed over me—I felt like I was moving backward. All I could picture was the sales gauntlet at Levitz Furniture. As the weekend progressed, I progressively convinced myself that attending the interview would waste everyone's time. I wasn't interested in going back to selling furniture.

On Monday morning, I called the headhunter to cancel the

appointment. "Look, Brad," he said. "He's already on his way over. Out of courtesy, could you come in and meet him?"

Despite my reservations, I replied, "If he's already on the way, sure. I'd be glad to meet him."

Little did I know that this seemingly random meeting would lead to significant personal and professional growth. It served as a reminder that sometimes the most unexpected opportunities can shape our future in ways we could never have imagined.

I have learned that timing is everything in our professional lives. But it's not just a matter of timing; it's about showing up and making the most of the opportunity. That's where the real magic happens. This realization has given me a sense of reassurance and confidence in my professional journey, knowing that success is within reach if I show up and seize the right opportunities.

Bill McMurry and his partner, Ed Stern, were not just selling furniture. They were the masterminds behind the Los Angeles distribution of Spacesaver, a product that was in a league of its own. Its unique selling point made it a well-known name in the industry. Their ability to adapt to any industry requirements set them apart in the sustainable storage and space industry. Its unique selling point made it a well-known name in the industry, guaranteeing a sale in any serious business organization. Being part of a team that distributed such a superior product was a significant step toward my financial independence.

This was also a tremendous learning opportunity. It wasn't just a step up; it elevated me to a different level. I interacted with professionals who had been in the business for years. I would visit their offices or go on site to review their bid requirements. Unlike my previous jobs, I didn't arrive with just a product; we would review their projects together. I would act as the project manager, complete the layouts and drawings, and review them with the architects. The architects would adapt them to Spacesaver specifications, and I would present them to the clients. When the bids went out, the request would specify the details of the system.

Bill and Ed ran a quarterly contest. They would alternate between the two of them, taking the person with the highest sales to dinner. When Bill took someone out to dinner, he would do it right. He genuinely enjoyed having a good time. I never felt that I was having dinner and drinks with my boss. I never felt uncomfortable or scrutinized. Bill had become my friend, and we'd worked hard to enjoy our dinners together.

It wasn't long before the two men discontinued alternating dinners. I remember Bill telling Ed, "Ed, I got Lieber. You take the Mormons."

The three Mormons to whom Bill referred were fellow salesmen, Scott Olpin, Jeff Nichols, and Brent Schetfield. Now, I have no bias against any religion. I don't ascribe to any, but what a person believes in or doesn't believe in is their business. I know this: these three made it very clear to everyone that religion was first, family second, and business third. I'd also heard that because of their religious beliefs, they weren't necessarily the life of the party.

My top sales performance often led to other rewards from Bill and his wife, Debbie, as well. When they took me to dinner, it wasn't just any restaurant. They would treat me to some of the most upscale locations in Southern California, particularly in San Clemente. These were not your average spots; they exuded luxury and exclusivity, making each visit a fascinating experience. I grew much closer to Bill than Ed. Ed was all business; I liked to have fun (some things never change).

What always impressed me about these guys was that they had money. Ed drove a big dually truck and pulled a big trailer with all the toys and the best amenities. Bill drove a '63 or '65 Corvette. They both lived in big new homes in San Clemente. I knew that was my future.

As the projects and money rolled in, my ambition for financial independence and business ownership grew stronger. Their success inspired me, and I became determined to achieve that level of prosperity. I worked smart, learning everything I could about the business, never shying away from hard work or the time required to accomplish the task—except on Friday afternoons.

I loved my job. I was as focused and dedicated as anyone could be when I was working. My commitment to working diligently, communicating with everyone involved, and keeping projects within budget and on time was crucial to our success. But I wasn't working on Friday afternoons. None of my customers worked on Friday afternoons, so attempting a sales call or corporate meeting then was pointless. So, every Friday, I would leave work early. I was still single, and Huntington Beach was a bachelor's playground. Friday afternoons were my time to beat the traffic and get to happy hour before the crowds to enjoy the beach and the company of friends. Having accomplished the critical parts of my job all week, I was committed to enjoying Friday afternoon happy hour!

It wasn't long before every Spacesaver, Los Angeles, employee recognized the benefits of working a half day on Fridays. I never realized how much my influence frustrated Ed.

Chapter 8
My One-and-Only Partner

The year was 1987. I was working with Spacesaver, Los Angeles, and one of my responsibilities was maintaining a presence at the meetings and gatherings of ARMA, the Area Records Manager's Association. ARMA was dedicated to connecting businesses through networking industry partners. One particular gathering was an evening dinner. As usual, I was the only representative of Spacesaver, Los Angeles, so I stood in line by myself.

I noticed her standing in line ahead of me. She didn't appear to be engaged in conversation with anyone, so I continued to watch. A few more minutes passed, and there was no sign of her being with anyone, so I left my place in line and approached her.

"Hi, my name is Brad Lieber. I'm with Spacesaver, Los Angeles." Her smile was captivating.

"Hello, Brad," she said. "I'm Janet Golman. I'm with Bell and Howell, Records Management."

I wasn't usually at a loss for words. However, at that moment they weren't coming to me as quickly as I was attempting to develop them.

"I'm here alone," I said, unsure why that would be an important statement.

"Oh, well, would you like to join our table?" Janet responded once again with the smile I'd first noticed. "I'm sure we can make room."

I was disappointed she was with a group but said, "Sure, I'd love to if it wouldn't be imposing."

"Not at all. These are my business associates," she continued as she introduced each of the individuals I was to be seated with during dinner.

Upon entering the restaurant, I followed the group to their table and took a seat. I soon found that I did not have to think of a topic to discuss during dinner—I became the topic.

"So, Brad, are you single?" the first person asked.

"Uh, yes, yes, I am single," I began. I was quickly interrupted by one of Janet's female associates.

"Janet is single," she generously offered. Janet's calm expression did not change.

"Are you Jewish?" another associate blurted out. Everyone laughed, but he was serious, and everyone was waiting for my answer.

"Well, yes. As a matter of fact, I am Jewish," I once again politely replied.

The same female associate chimed in again, "Janet's Jewish!"

The rest of the dinner is a blur to me now. I know we exchanged business cards and phone numbers. I had every intention of calling her but waited a week or two. I didn't want to appear too eager, and I suppose I didn't want to hear her say she was too busy. There was something very different about this woman, something I sensed I did not want to lose.

Janet was single and Jewish, and so was I. We were in similar industries and knew a lot of the same people. Janet was very well-established—and I was broke. This posed a very serious challenge for me. I might be able to take her out occasionally, but certainly not as much as I would have liked or to the places I would have preferred to take her. But there was something very special about this woman, and I did not want her to slip away from me.

After a few dates, I finally had to come clean about my situation. I explained that I enjoyed being together and wanted to spend more time with her, but I couldn't afford it. Once again, Janet was unfazed. She immediately came up with a solution.

"Brad, you'll sign a note with me for a thousand dollars," she said. "It will be our dating money."

I'd never heard of such a thing, but then, I'd never met a woman like Janet.

I signed a thousand-dollar note, borrowing the money to date her and, therefore, spend more time together.

Fortunately, my mom and dad had taken a one-thousand-dollar life insurance policy on me and each of my brothers. I cashed in the policy and paid her back. It remains the most rewarding business transaction of my entire life.

Our relationship grew quickly. It wasn't long before Janet took me home to introduce me to her mom and dad. Her dad scared the shit out of me. He wasn't a menacing person; it was his business acumen that was so intimidating. He was the picture of success—*real* success. LeRoy Golman was brilliant.

Eli Broad had worked as a junior accountant for Janet's dad. He left the company and partnered with Don Kaufman to launch Kaufman and Broad Building Company in 1957, eleven years after World War II ended. Young families were searching for affordable homes, and Kaufman and Broad developed an ingenious method of constructing slab homes that were affordable for first-time buyers.

Eli contacted Janet's dad and told him Kaufman and Broad needed him to control the financial end of their business as the number three executive in the corporation. It was LeRoy Golman, Janet's dad and my future father-in-law, who listed what is now known as KB Home on the New York Stock Exchange in 1969. They were the first homebuilders ever to be listed.

Janet was used to being taken to dinner. She now found herself hanging out with a guy who had to sign a note for dating money. I knew this woman was too sharp to make a mistake. Her faith in me gave me all the more confidence in myself.

Like everything else in my life, our relationship was unconventional. I met Janet when I wasn't looking for love, but she quickly became an integral part of my life. I knew I loved her, but we hadn't discussed marriage in detail. Sure, the subject came up, but it was somewhere in the future—until we decided to get an apartment together in Marina Del Rey.

Her dad was helping us get the apartment set up. He and I were putting shelving paper down. Now, one would think that I would be considering asking him for his daughter's hand in marriage, you know, the conventional way. But LeRoy beat me to the punch.

Out of nowhere, he bluntly said, "Why don't you just get married?"

His question caught me off guard, a twist in the narrative that I hadn't anticipated.

"Huh?" It was the only thing that left my lips.

LeRoy repeated himself. "You're living together. Why don't you just get married?"

I was still struggling to offer him an appropriate response, but nothing was coming to mind. I didn't offer him our plans; we hadn't made any. I didn't say anything that might lead him to believe this was something we'd been discussing.

So, I did what any man would do in my position. I sheepishly responded, "Okay."

Now, I was in a bind. I still wasn't making enough money to purchase a ring. Hell, I'd just been making enough to share in the rent of our apartment. So, I called my dad, who contacted a cousin in the jewelry business. My dad got a ring from him and sent it to me.

One morning, in our apartment, without any grand gestures or elaborate plans, I asked Janet, "What would you think about marrying me?"

I'd stopped Janet in her tracks. She tilted her head slightly and gave me that smile I found captivating when we first met, followed by a very serious look.

"Are you asking me?" she responded.

I said, "Yeah, I'm asking you."

We are a lot alike. Her response to me was the same as my response to her dad, "Okay." It was a moment of mutual understanding and agreement, a testament to our shared values and perspectives.

Janet and I were married on January 16, 1988. It was a day filled with joy and love, a celebration of our commitment to each other.

We enjoyed our beautiful apartment overlooking the yachts in Marina Del Rey together. I was still working for Spacesaver, Los Angeles (only half a day on Fridays), but it was now Janet with whom I would spend my free time. My bachelor days were forever gone, and a new chapter of shared responsibilities and joys began.

I was doing okay with Ed and Bill, but I wanted more. I wanted the lifestyle they were enjoying. That desire came up in conversation with Scott Olpin, one of the three Mormons, who had mentioned his goal to one day have his own business.

As time passed, our discussions became more focused and intentional. While I was serious, Scott seemed hesitant to make a move. I finally asked him why he was reluctant. He mentioned that he'd received an inquiry from ACME Visible Records, an office storage and file systems specialist, which was headquartered in Virginia. ACME had secretly approached the three Mormons and wanted to recruit them away from Ed and Bill to open a division in Los Angeles.

Scott was a nice guy, but he was more interested in talking with ACME than pursuing a business relationship with me. At that point, I figured ACME was anybody's game, so I called them.

"One moment, sir. I'll see if Mr. Titsworth is available," the voice on the other end of the phone responded. They returned a moment later. "Thank you for holding, sir. I'll put you through to Mr. Titsworth."

"Hello, this is Mike Titsworth. To whom am I speaking?"

"Hello, Mr. Titsworth," I replied. "My name is Brad Lieber. I work for Spacesaver, Los Angeles."

"Hello, Mr. Lieber. And what has prompted your call?" Titsworth asked.

"Sir, I understand your company is considering opening distribution in Southern California, and that you've contacted my co-workers here at Spacesaver."

"I see." There was a momentary pause. "Well, we are interested in expanding into the Southern California market," he said.

"Look, Mr. Titsworth. Can I be totally honest with you?" I asked.

"I wish you would," Titsworth replied.

"You're trying to recruit three Mormons. I have nothing against Mormons, absolutely nothing. But think about it. You are trying to recruit three Mormons to start a new business. I know these fellas. For them, it's religion first, family second, and business third." I paused to see if he would respond. He did not, so I continued. "Mr. Titsworth, I'm a hungry Jew. I'm your man!"

My blunt comment was met with a light chuckle. "Excuse me, what did you say your first name is?" he asked.

"Brad. Brad Lieber," I replied.

He chuckled, then said, "Brad, you may have a point. I think we need to talk a bit further. Do you have time now?"

"Absolutely. You're my only priority at the moment."

We talked in detail, after which Mike told me he was flying to meet me in person from Virginia. Little did I know our meeting would be a formality. He'd made his decision during our initial telephone conversation.

It was like meeting someone I'd known all my life when we met. Mike pulled no punches. He was direct and to the point.

"Brad, I'm going to put you in business!" he said as he reached forward to shake my hand.

And that is precisely what he did. ACME Visible Records offered me a non-recoverable $80,000 draw annually for my first three years—I was in business!

The first order of business was to let Ed and Bill know that I would be leaving Spacesaver, Los Angeles, and going to work for ACME. I knew they would be upset. After all, I'd been a good salesman for them. Bill and I were especially close. They'd no doubt discussed plans for me and my future with their business.

I loaded my files, notes, and Spacesaver equipment into the back of my car.

When I arrived, I was immediately notified that Ed wanted to see me in his office. Ed and Bill were not just my bosses; they had also become my mentors and friends. I knew it would be a shock, but now was as good a time as any to let them know I'd decided to leave their company. It wasn't an easy decision, but I felt that it was time for me to move on and explore new opportunities. I had nothing against either of the men; it was just a personal decision.

I was correct. It was time for me to leave.

It was shocking, to say the least, but not in the way I had planned. Evidently, Ed's frustration with my taking off early for happy hour on Friday afternoons had reached a tipping point. The funny thing was, I wasn't a big drinker. I couldn't tell the difference between a Château Lafite Rothschild and a bottle of Mad Dog. I just wanted to beat the traffic and be where the fun took place. I suppose the thing that pissed Ed off the most was my influence over the other employees. Because of me, everyone was now leaving work early on Friday afternoons—even the three Mormons!

I was unceremoniously fired, which left me in a momentary state of shock. I couldn't believe what was happening. I got up, went out to my car, brought in every item representing my work with Spacesaver, Los Angeles, including a few paperclips and a stapler, and politely said, "Here's my shit."

They never asked why my car was loaded with all their supplies.

A year or so after my departure, the salespeople pitched an idea to Ed to buy Bill out of the company. Bill, always open to new opportunities, thought it might be a good time to make a move.

Selling all or a portion of a business is not a decision to be taken lightly. It requires detailed planning and careful consideration of all parties involved. In this case, they had to discuss the intricacies of their partnership and how to ensure a smooth transition of Bill's responsibilities, which were the nuts and bolts of the business, to those remaining after his departure. Ed, being the detail-oriented administrator, also recognized the need for a line of succession in the event of a catastrophic event that might incapacitate him from performing his duties. His primary concern was ensuring financial protection for his wife, Linda.

After a series of discussions with Ed, followed by legal discussions with his attorney and financial adviser, Bill agreed to the sale of his portion of the business. The deal was closed on a Friday evening. Ed completed the insurance forms that would protect Linda's future in case of a catastrophic event. He would send in the forms on Monday morning.

Just two days later, on Sunday, Ed passed away from a sudden heart attack. The insurance forms he had intended to mail remained in his desk drawer until employees later discovered them. His death left his wife, Linda, unexpectedly responsible for running the business.

Witnessing this from afar, I determined such an event would never happen to Janet.

Danny "Dutch" Gladys   Anne and LeRoy Golman

Check Number 1075 in Janet's Check Register.
The loan she gave me so that I could afford to date her.

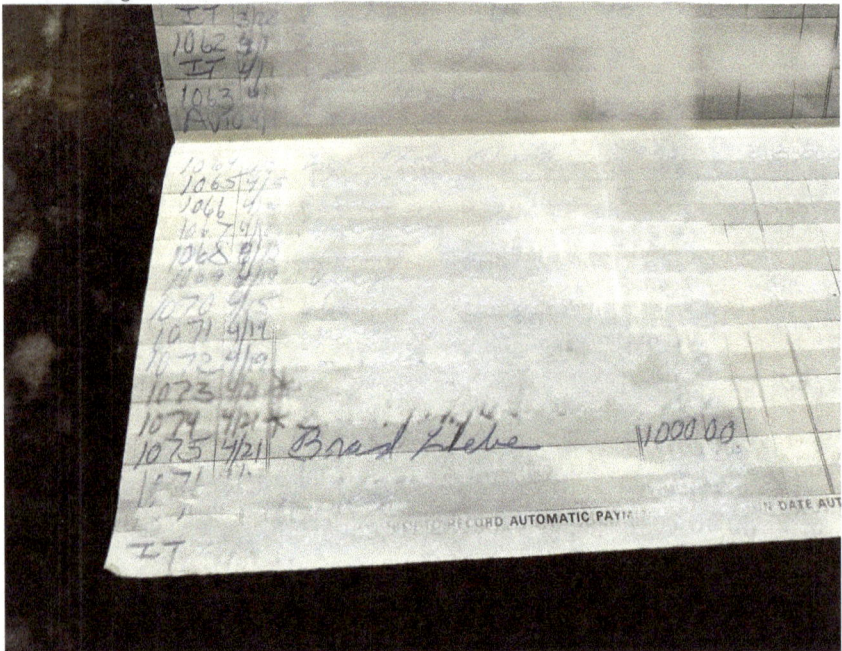

January 16, 1988, Our wedding day

Chapter 9
ACME Visible Records -
Lieber and Associates

When ACME Visible Records was in search of a distributor in Southern California, I seized the opportunity and transitioned into the role. ACME's offer to set me up in my own business was a turning point, and Lieber and Associates became a reality. The future was filled with promise, and I was thrilled to see my efforts pay off. As promised, I received a generous monthly compensation, and I was able to expand ACME's business in Southern California. My Rolodex was brimming with the names and numbers of architects, general contractors, and business owners throughout the region, a testament to the connections I had built.

Lieber and Associates, located in Van Nuys, California, was now exclusively selling ACME's color-coded folders and high-density mobile shelving. Having distributed office equipment for Copy R and Monroe Systems and having built a positive reputation because of my commitment to clients' needs, I was given the first opportunity to present my new line of products to my former clients. I did so, however, as the owner of Lieber and Associates.

My journey was a testament to the value of self-education in business. I'd found myself; I was in my niche and owned my own business.

What could go wrong? I'd learned it all, and while establishing myself in the industry and building a fledgling company, I'd secured my C-61 Limited Specialty Contractor license, which allowed me to perform specialized construction services. I also earned B-24 and C-24 certifications, which allowed me to act as a subcontractor to the general contractors I worked with. These credentials were not just a means to an end but a path to expanded opportunities and unlimited money. The C-61 license, for instance, allowed me to take on more specialized projects, increasing my revenue potential. The B-24 and C-24 certifications enabled me to work with larger contractors, opening doors to bigger projects and more significant profits.

Janet and I moved out of our apartment in Marina Del Rey and into a single-level, 2,000-square-foot cinder block home in Van Nuys. From our 270-square-foot guest house, Janet and I, along with her cousin, Emily, began Lieber and Associates.

My father-in-law, LeRoy, decided our little guest house office needed some music. "Brad, why don't you at least buy a radio and brighten this place up?" he suggested.

I countered, "I don't have $100 to spend on a radio. I'm trying to build a business." I impressed myself with my thrift until LeRoy continued.

"Just expense it to the business," he said.

Puzzled, I looked at him. "Just what?" I asked.

"Expense it," he repeated. "Let the business buy the radio."

So, without letting LeRoy know, I had no idea what he was talking about, I learned what expense reporting for the business was all about.

I learned a tremendous amount from my father-in-law. He taught me about finances, sound business principles, and common-sense practices that made a huge difference in developing a successful company.

Our wedding brought together two families that genuinely enjoyed one another's company. Sandy, LeRoy's brother, was particularly interested in my endeavors. One day, we were sitting together, having a cocktail. Sandy was undoubtedly enjoying a Rob Roy when my father-in-law turned to him and said, "Sandy, Bradley doesn't need income. He knows how to get that." Sandy and I leaned forward, anticipating my father-in-law's words of wisdom. "Bradley needs to build wealth!"

Those words stuck with me. They marked a turning point in my understanding of business and success. It wasn't just about making money; it was about creating lasting wealth and value. This perspective shaped my decision-making and strategic thinking from that point on.

My journey to success would no longer be random. I strategically pursued opportunities, always with the mindset of building wealth or planning a timely exit. In every instance, I carefully considered the needs of potential clients and how best to serve them. Each client was not just a customer but a potential marketing partner for Lieber and Associates. I focused on architects, designers, and individuals shaping buildings and offices. I saved them design time by providing them with our product specifications and ensuring our products met their architectural standards.

By networking with architects, designers, and general managers, I removed potential delays, completed our work quietly and efficiently, and allowed them to focus on addressing any issues that inevitably arose elsewhere. Lieber and Associates was committed to problem-solving. Once we completed a job, we became their insurance policy against concerns. We were not concerned about the competition. When we secured a client, we became part of a greater team effort. Every job we were awarded became an assurance of future business. The company was my pot of gold on the path to wealth; it was time to get on my knees and begin paving!

Lieber and Associates contracted with hospital medical records and radiology departments in Southern California. A significant portion of our growth, however, was with law firms and the Hollywood studios. The broadening of our influence in several industries solidified our reputation and further expanded our reach.

Lieber and Associates had not quite reached its first anniversary when Janet announced she was pregnant. I would be a father. It was a very exciting time for us and the entire family, but it was also a time of uncertainty. The business was still in its early stages, and we were facing the typical challenges of a new venture. I was sitting alone, pondering the wonderful news, realizing that I would soon be taking on the role my father had assumed when I was born, when the thought occurred to me, "Holy shit, would my kid be like me?" Would he or she be a payback for what my mom and dad went through raising me? It was a sobering consideration.

We had a very smooth pregnancy. For the most part, we continued working as we had been without interruption. I was as cool as a cucumber when Janet's labor pains began. As the pains increased and grew closer together, my calm and collected demeanor began to waver.

"Brad, get my things," Janet finally said. "We need to go to the hospital now." Her tone was calm but firm. She was in total control. She presented no signs of concern and no misgivings about what was soon to take place. On the other hand, I was not necessarily her source of strength.

She reviewed the items she needed to prepare for her trip to Cedar Sinai Hospital.

"What's that?" I asked.

"Oh, that's the medication the doctor told me to take before we leave." Janet paused and flicked her wrist, saying, "I'm not going to take that."

"What is it?" I once again asked.

"Oh, it's Nembutal. It's supposed to calm me down before—"

I interrupted, "Here, give me that. I'll take it!" I knew what it was: pentobarbital, a yellow jacket.

From what I remember, things were peaceful throughout Janet's labor. In the delivery room, the doctor and I casually discussed our favorite sushi bars, only occasionally interrupted by Janet's need for assistance. He asked Janet what her degree of pain was. I told him I was not having any.

Finally, Janet called out to the doctor, "Doctor, I think I am dilating."

The doctor and I both responded, "Breathe."

The doctor invited me to wait in the adjacent waiting room, which I did. Moments later, the door opened, and the doctor announced, "Mr. Lieber, you have a beautiful daughter!"

And that she was, as she remains today! Dana was perfect in every way. I was so proud of Janet and grateful for the wonderful gift of life she'd given me.

As our first child, Dana became the practice run for a future addition. Janet was a natural; I was not so much. I remember she needed some time for herself shortly after bringing the baby home. She went to have her nails done, leaving me home alone with Dana. After that, Janet decided it was far less stressful to stay home than answer the telephone every few minutes while I fired another volley of questions about how to do something.

I did, however, learn. Dana became my original "sushi baby," a term I coined for her. I would put her in her car seat, drive to one of the many sushi bars that the doctor who delivered her and I had discussed, sit her on the counter, and enjoy sushi. It was there that Dirk Benedict and I met. Dirk was the good-looking actor who played Face on the *A-Team* television program. He loved sushi and took a real liking to Dana.

Ryan's birth two years later, at Encino-Tarzana Hospital, went relatively easily for me. As I remember the event, it was pretty much a duplicate of Dana's birth. I remember, however, when the doctor told me, "Mr. Lieber, you have a son," I immediately thought, "One of each. Mission accomplished!"

You'd think we had it made with a new baby, a new business, and a new home. However, the reality was different. Dana came home with no directions. There was nothing to explain what her crying meant. Was she hungry? Did she need to be changed? Was she hurting somewhere? Was she just playing me? I didn't know, and I didn't want to reinforce something that would encourage her to cry for no reason. Janet seemed to think I was making too much out of the situation. If she'd just eaten, she wasn't hungry. If she needed to have her diaper changed, check her diaper and change it if it needed changing. If there was no apparent cause for discomfort, I was probably being played, and she wanted to be held. More often than not, I fell for it.

Time has a way of adjusting our lives, and as time progresses, so does technology. Technology can be a blessing for those whose jobs are simplified because of it. Those corporations that, with advancements in technology, increase their efficiencies and therefore increase their profits. However, technology can be a curse for those who built their businesses in response to customer needs prior to their technological advancements. For me, it served as yet another call to action. Hospital radiology departments were shifting to PAC systems and from their medical records departments to online programs. Lieber and Associates solidified its position with law firms, establishing our presence in central file rooms and libraries. It was a challenging journey, but we persevered.

My fledgling company successfully adapted to the unpredictable nature of evolving business technologies. We were dedicated to providing our clients with proactive options in systems and services, which led to our 1994 nomination for the prestigious Calibre Design Award, the highest recognition within our industry.

The nomination gave Lieber and Associates credibility. The award banquet was a black-tie event at the Fairmont Century Plaza Hotel. My parents flew out, Janet's parents were there, and we had a special table reserved for the nominees and their families. It was the Oscars of the industry!

I found it equally exciting and humbling. I was thrilled to see the look in my parents' eyes. Their pride and their long-awaited relief that their youngest son had found his niche—and was being recognized for his success in it—were worth more to me than any trophy could have been. There we were, a small company composed of three people, being recognized alongside Steelcase Furniture, Hayworth Office Furniture, and Herman Miller, each a well-established corporation and a major player in the furniture industry. This was a big deal, and it made us all feel like we were part of something bigger.

Following dinner, the master of ceremonies took the stage to extol the virtues of this recognition. He recognized each of our businesses for their quality, commitment, and contribution to the industry. We sat politely, preparing to smile and applaud the award's recipient.

"The 1994 winner of the prestigious Calibre Design Award goes to—"

There was a momentary pause as he opened the envelope. I'd been staring at my lap where my folded hands, moist with perspiration, were preparing to applaud. I looked up for a moment into my father's eyes. He was staring back at me, through me. His gaze was one of pride and long-held confidence. I remember his quiet smile as he ever-so-slightly nodded. In that moment, a rush of emotions and thoughts flooded my mind. I thought about the hard work, the sacrifices, and the support of my family that led to this moment.

The master of ceremonies flipped open the card, which had been secured in a sealed envelope, and announced the name of the 1994 recipient: "LIEBER AND ASSOCIATES!"

My jaw dropped. Cameras flashed, bright lights flooded the room, and our table was engulfed in the spotlight of recognition. Everyone stood. My family applauded. There were hugs and tears as my family patted me on the back and urged me to take the stage. It was a magnificent feeling of accomplishment, one that filled us all with pride and satisfaction.

It's funny how in the middle of an out-of-body experience, brought on by an unanticipated, life-changing event, a small, seemingly insignificant detail caught my attention.

There I was—me—on stage. All the cameras were focused on me, little Bradley Lieber. The kid from Monessen. The kid with more attempts at education and fewer educational successes than probably any other individual in the room. As I looked up at the screen capturing the event, something was missing. It was, to borrow a phrase from ABC's Wide World of Sports, the thrill of victory, the agony of defeat. As the cameras zoomed in on me, they captured an unmistakable bald spot. I'm not talking about thinning hair or a misplaced comb-over. I'd developed a pronounced bald spot that I'd never seen before. No one had ever mentioned it, not even Janet!

This unexpected detail added a touch of reality and humility to the surreal moment. I was still Bradley Lieber, with all my imperfections. More importantly, there was still much more to accomplish.

Chapter 10
Ownership

When you own a business that exclusively represents another company headquartered across the United States, you do not participate in that company's corporate discussions. All I knew was that Lieber and Associates was fulfilling its part of the agreement with ACME Visible Records, and we were making money—a lot of money! It should have been a win-win situation for ACME and us since I was making a lot of money moving a lot of their products. ACME did not see it quite the same way. To them, I was double-dipping. I was receiving the $80,000 non-recoverable draw as we'd agreed, but I was also making much more from the profit of my company. They'd under-estimated me.

The president of ACME Visible Records, Tom Fontana, came to California to talk. We visited briefly; however, his trip was not simply to have a casual conversation. I don't know what it was about him that was off-putting to me. Perhaps it was his suspenders; I've always been cautious of guys wearing suspenders.

"Look, Brad. I can't keep this deal going the way we originally planned," he said and then paused for a moment. "It looks like you are doing pretty well."

I agreed. I was doing very well. Without getting deep into the details, Tom explained what was happening at corporate and how it would impact my division in Southern California. Through his nervous double-talk, the real purpose of Tom's visit became clear to me. ACME had decided it could not sustain its presence in California.

"You understand," he concluded.

I didn't understand at all, but I'd found that in business, as in life, it doesn't pay to waste time worrying about things. Worry is simply a call to action. It signals that something needs to be addressed, a problem must be solved. Do you want to eliminate worry and stress? Then do whatever it takes to correct the situation. This proactive approach to problem-solving has been a guiding principle in my business journey. It's not our problems but how we address them that truly matters. This approach has empowered me to navigate the challenges in my professional life.

Without hesitation, I said, "I appreciate the opportunity your company has given me to start my own business."

I knew that I held all the cards. Our contract was for three years, with a non-recoverable draw of $80,000 annually. Lieber and Associates had only represented ACME Visible Records for a year and a half. In that year and a half, our company was awarded the prestigious Calibre Design Award and built a strong presence in Southern California. I'd done my part. Breaching a contractual agreement was not in ACME's best interest.

So I continued, "Tom, if you could pay me for the next three months, it would give my company time to make the necessary adjustments." This request was not a sign of desperation but a strategic move to ensure the smooth transition of my business. It was a decision made with a sense of control and reassurance in the face of uncertainty.

There was clear relief in Tom's demeanor. "No problem, Brad," he said. "I'll pay you $7,000 per month for three months. After that, Lieber and Associates will be on its own."

I contacted Advanced Manufacturing Company, a Southern California group in Gardena, California. Advanced produced high-density mobile shelving. I'd been aware that their product was considered aesthetically substandard in the industry. A careful analysis revealed why. They'd cut corners that, in the long run, had cost them. They'd used inferior paint, and as a result, the appearance of their work negatively reflected on them and their customers' businesses.

Lieber and Associates identified the problem and offered an alternative. We decided to invest in a higher-quality paint that would not only improve the look of the shelving but also increase its durability. Additionally, we upgraded the rails in all moving parts, improving the product's functionality and longevity. ACME Visible Records was no longer visible. Lieber and Associates was moving on.

Chapter 11
The Value of a Good Name

T he Lieber name and reputation have always been essential to me. They embody my parents' unwavering confidence in me, even as I pursued an unconventional path. Their belief in my potential was a source of pride and a profound gift for which I am forever grateful.

I now owned my own business, and despite the challenges posed by my suppliers' turmoil, Lieber and Associates consistently landed on its feet. These challenges, from sudden changes in supply to financial uncertainties, tested our resilience and determination. But each time, we emerged stronger, more adaptable, and more determined to succeed.

Advanced Manufacturing Company, having adopted the corrective actions we had proposed, began upgrading its systems. This improvement enhanced their reputation within the high-density mobile shelving industry. As a result, Lieber and Associates became the sole distributor for Advanced, further increasing our impact in Southern California.

It had been a while since I had treated myself to a new car, and the joy of the purchase was unparalleled. As a family man now, I chose a stunning Lexus LS400, gold with a tan interior. The luxury and spaciousness of the car, along with its ability to block out all external noise when the windows were up, were a true delight. The comfortable spring, strut, and shock combination made every California pothole a non-issue, ensuring a smooth, enjoyable ride.

Our company's growth did not go unnoticed. In the latter part of November 1993, I received a call from Interiors, Northern California's Spacesaver distributor in Sacramento. This call would forever change my life, my family, and the lives of many individuals I hadn't yet met. It was not just about a potential business opportunity but a validation of my hard work, recognition of my reputation, and the beginning of a new chapter in my entrepreneurial journey.

"Brad, it's Jim Bunt, Interiors, in Sacramento. I'm glad I got a hold of you. How are you doing?" he asked.

"I'm doing fine, Jim," I said. "I haven't heard from you in a long time. How are things up in Sacramento?"

He ignored my question and continued, "I know you are doing fine, Brad; everyone knows. That brings me to the reason for my call." He paused briefly to gather his thoughts. "Brad, the Spacesaver team in San Francisco is experiencing financial trouble. If you're interested, I can connect you with Bill Wettstein, the Executive Vice President of Spacesaver. It might be a great opportunity for you. I think I can help you secure the line."

Spacesaver has always been the Mercedes-Benz of the high-density mobile storage industry. It remains years ahead of anything else on the market and is known for its technologically advanced motorized units, impeccable design, and craftsmanship. Whenever you name a company whose products have enviable name recognition within its industry, Spacesaver is mentioned. For me, it represented my pot of gold at the end of the rainbow, a symbol of quality and excellence.

I thanked Jim for his call. Of course, I understood its importance, and when I hung up, the intensity of the opportunity began to stir something within me. This was it. I had been working toward this; it had been my dream.

For the first time in my life, I began methodically considering the steps I had to take to prepare myself and my family for such a move: selling our home, selling our business, relocating, finding a home in the San Francisco Bay Area, introducing myself to current clients, and meeting new potential clients. And then it occurred to me—first, I had to call Bill Wettstein.

I allowed the importance of the call to sink in and my nervous anticipation to settle down, and then I called him the next day. Bill remembered me and made it a special point to tell me that he did. He said he would fly out to the San Francisco Bay Area in two days and would like to meet me at the Spacesaver office in Hercules, California. The call evoked a mix of excitement, nervousness, and a deep sense of responsibility.

The meeting was set. I needed only to purchase my airline ticket and show up. Janet's excitement increased mine even more. She knew with the Spacesaver account, there was no limit to the success we could enjoy together.

Two days later, I walked into the Hercules office and was met by Mr. Bill Wettstein, the Executive Vice President of Spacesaver. His warm smile immediately struck me. He was an impressive, soft-spoken man who embodied a savvy professionalism that I was immediately attracted to.

"Brad, it's a pleasure to meet you finally," he said as he shook my hand. "Thank you for coming up here to chat."

"Bill, thank you for the opportunity," I replied, still shaking his hand and enjoying the genuineness of his smile.

Bill showed me around the office. We discussed the present clientele and the industries they represented. With Silicon Valley so close, it seemed odd that their present location was sixty miles away. I controlled my exuberance and listened to what Bill had to share. He did not make that easy. He was far more interested in listening to what I had to say. I never got the impression it was to judge me or my answers. He was genuinely interested in my opinion. Without formally joining forces, we were already discussing the opportunities and what it would take to complete the company's intended expansion.

We had lunch and spent the entire day together. It was a perfect day.

I asked Bill what the debt was, and he told me $300,000. When I offered him a deal of $100,000 for three years, which he accepted, I knew the weight of the responsibility that came with it. On December 1, 1993, as I signed a note at 1% and expressed my readiness to represent the Spacesaver line, I could feel the gravity of the situation. Bill's confidence in me was palpable, and it was as if a burden had been lifted from his shoulders. We shook hands, and that warm Wisconsin smile welcomed me into a dream relationship with the leading high-density mobile storage industry manufacturer.

The move would be a new beginning. Once I was awarded the Spacesaver product line, it was lights out. I could sell their products in Sioux Falls, South Dakota, in the dead of winter—and Janet, my pillar of support, would be there without hesitation. All I had to do was say, "Hi, I'm Brad Lieber. I'm your Spacesaver guy!" The name recognition said it all.

Over the years, my team has added to that recognition: quality people, environment, business, products, and service. As an owner, you must be willing to invest in building a business, not just a product line. This practice ensured yet unseen business expansion.

Each phase of my work experience in Southern California added to the last. I knew my competition, their weaknesses, and that, in most cases, I could go in with 25% to 30% margins and still be less expensive than them. I also made it a point to know my potential clients, their vulnerabilities, and their competitors' strengths.

I discovered that listening was the most powerful tool in my business arsenal. My conversations with architects and designers often echoed from one company to the next. This repetition reinforced my understanding and my ability to discuss their goals effectively and intelligently.

When I was awarded the bid, I would partner with the client to forecast future requirements, and I would enhance their experience by suggesting additional services and products that would allow them to grow in preparation for their anticipated expansions.

Northern California was a new territory I knew very little about. While the industries were the same, personalities, workforces, distances, and business cultures differed. While Spacesaver was at the top of the line in Northern California, Brad Lieber was unknown. It would be my responsibility to assure the current client base and potential clients that the Lieber name stood for higher quality, greater dependability, and better service than they'd formerly experienced. It would be my responsibility to complement and enhance the quality and dependability the industry had grown to expect from the product I was now representing.

I immediately called Janet from my new office in Hercules, California, and shared the good news with her: The Liebers were on the move! Janet, as always, never doubted. While she was thrilled beyond words, her response was knowing and calm. Of course, we were progressing, and of course, this move would lead to greater success.

On my return flight to Burbank, I made a mental list of the first things I needed to do:

1. Begin shutting down Lieber and Associates
2. Find a qualified suitor to maintain our Southern California customer base and assume potential clients we were approaching
3. Sell our home
4. Establish a place in Northern California to temporarily live while traveling back and forth for the remainder of our six-month lease on our Southern California home
5. Create a new business name and corporation
6. Change my logo and letterhead to our new business name and location
7. Negotiate a rental deal for an automobile in Northern California

8. Stabilize our Bay Area presence and expand it where possible
9. Plan intentional time with my wife and kids to let them know that I was present, and they were first in my life
10. And, ultimately get rid of that fucking bald spot!

Chapter 12
Making the Move

When I contacted Bill McMurry and extended Lieber and Associates' contacts to him, it marked a pivotal moment. Our bond had endured the test of time—even after my departure from Spacesaver, Los Angeles. I had complete confidence in Bill's ability to nurture our clients and prospects. His offer of $15,000 was equitable, and I readily accepted it. That business's value paled when compared to the promising opportunities that lay ahead in Northern California.

Having sold the business to Bill, I now had to arrange my part-time living in the Bay Area while Janet, Dana, and Ryan would still live in Van Nuys. I decided to fly Southwest Airlines from Burbank to the Oakland International Airport every Sunday or Monday and return every Friday. Southwest offered a frequent flier program that allowed me to get coupons for a free flight every six weeks. I got a similar deal from Budget Car Rental in Oakland with a free week after every eight rentals. Of course, these were all business expenses; LeRoy had taught me well.

The Emeryville Holiday Inn became my temporary residence, another business expense. During my six-month stay, I became friends with every worker there. They all spoke Spanish, and I never understood a word they said, yet they must have thought I was their most grateful customer. They would rattle off something in Spanish, and I would smile and proudly respond, "Gracias!" Their kindness and hospitality were constant reminders of the importance of humility and appreciation in business.

It became clear that strategic personnel changes were necessary and imperative at Hercules. In any business, it's not just about employees understanding the company's values but also about embodying them. It's about fostering a connection with the company's heart, message, and mission. These changes were not just about individuals but about the company's strategic direction.

Successful businesses are not only about the products or services they offer. They are collaborative movements of engaged individuals committed to doing their best and sharing in each other's success. Each individual's contribution either adds value or subtracts value. There is no middle ground. You are either filling a vital part of the business or taking away from it.

When I purchased Spacesaver of Northern California, I was starting a new business. I named it Systems & Space, Incorporated because that was exactly what we excelled in, providing clients with increased storage capacity. For the most part, my new employees considered our company a job. One individual stood out among the eight employees who had been part of Spacesaver of Northern California. Andy, a remarkable figure, had been the acting sales manager. His extensive knowledge, higher education, and unwavering passion made him an invaluable asset to the team. The company's success was a direct reflection of his dedication to service. Andy remained with me through the transition and well into the beginnings of our new growth.

Spacesaver was—and still is—the best product in the industry. Having Andy on board was a significant advantage. He had established essential contacts within the industry that would serve as a springboard for our further expansion. His character was commendable, noteworthy for his selflessness. He understood that I would lead our sales efforts and was comfortable stepping back to assume a more supportive role in our collaborative efforts.

Back in Van Nuys, I focused on selling our home. Over the years, I had made quite a few improvements—perhaps too many. It would take the perfect buyer, someone willing to pay well above market price, for me to break even. I couldn't imagine that happening and often wondered what earth-shaking event might occur to prevent us from losing too much money on the sale.

On January 17, 1994, the day after Janet and I celebrated our sixth wedding anniversary, a magnitude 6.7 earthquake in Northridge rocked the San Fernando Valley. It was eight seconds of the most powerful quake since 1971. Our home sustained damage—though not severe, it was enough to put us in a seemingly greater financial bind. However, after meeting with our banker, the bank agreed to accept the home in its current condition. This unexpected turn of events was a huge relief that spared us from further costs or liabilities. We emerged from the situation financially unscathed, feeling the weight of the financial burden lifted off our shoulders.

The movers carefully loaded our furniture into their moving van while Dana, Fah, and I prepared for the five-hour trip to the San Francisco Bay Area. Fah was Dana's plush toy fox. They were inseparable.

The drive up Interstate 5 has not changed over the years. After passing through the Grapevine, your mind braces for the long stretch of nothingness ahead. Then you remember Coalinga. Roll up the windows, close the vents, turn up the air conditioning, and increase your speed to numbers that would impress Indy 500 race car drivers. Not even the hermetically sealed windows of my LS400 could protect us. There is absolutely nothing that can comfort you while driving through the stench of bovine excrement in Coalinga, California. When you finally get through to the outskirts, rolling down the windows hits you with one last blast from the stubborn odor that seems to have clung to your car, waiting for you to crack open a window. Even the look on Fah's face was momentarily altered with disgust!

Besides the occasional potty break, there was no reason to stop anywhere along Interstate 5. Dana and I arrived in Danville and stayed at a hotel until Janet, Ryan, and our furniture arrived, allowing us to settle into our new home together.

As you grow a business, you encounter various phases of change. The industries you serve are constantly evolving, requiring you to adjust to accommodate new requirements, regulations, and technologies. These are standard and expected developments for every business. However, there are also unique changes that may be specific to your industry and clientele, such as shifts in consumer preferences or market dynamics. Understanding and adapting to this evolution is crucial for the success of your business.

Another critical aspect of change involves personal circumstances that affect your employees. Divorce, health issues, or family emergencies can significantly impact their productivity, commitment, and loyalty. Ideally, a stable job should be a constant source of support in their lives, but this stability is often underestimated and, unfortunately, overlooked. Tensions can also arise from inflated egos, particularly from individuals who believe their influence is the sole reason for the company's success.

This brings me to another essential truth I have learned as a business owner: people have the power to hire and fire themselves. What I mean by this is that employees ultimately decide their fate within the company. Their actions, performance, and attitude determine whether they continue to be a part of our team—I simply inform them of their decision.

As Systems & Space expanded, each new client and industry propelled us to greater opportunities and further expansion. Our successes, which were a direct result of the team's hard work and dedication, did not go unnoticed. By our sixth year in Pleasanton, the office was bursting at the seams. Relocation was an absolute necessity. On June 1, 1999, we moved to our present location, just a short distance from the first. The newness, the freshness, and the camaraderie were electric!

After eight years with us, three in Los Angeles and five in the San Francisco Bay Area, Janet's cousin, Emily, moved out of state to pursue her dreams. We'd experienced significant financial growth since Emily joined us. It was now necessary to hire an experienced accountant to handle the books.

When you consider the intricate architectural, engineering, construction, and product management required to run our business successfully, it is surprising that the most indispensable part of the company was accounting. While other employees are humming with excitement about designing and constructing customer requirements, the accounting department is crunching numbers. Day in and day out, they focus on numbers. I couldn't do it. My financial understanding might have appeared simplistic, but I knew my costs and the volume of business necessary to cover my direct and indirect expenses, payroll, taxes, insurance, and inventory. I relied on my financial team to maintain the specifics.

I began interviewing people for the position. Accounting is not an area where you want to see high turnover. I finally hired someone who appeared promising. She had a terrific résumé, showed up with enthusiasm to join our company, and seemed to be a perfect fit. Her reason for leaving the company, however, confused me. She'd traveled from San Jose to Pleasanton for her original interview and for training. She'd worked for a couple of weeks without any inkling of dissatisfaction. She then notified me that she would not continue her employment with Systems & Space because the distance between her home and our office was too far.

This left me with the task of once again interviewing. I met with everyone sent to me from every agency. I felt like that was all that I was doing! I'd had enough. It came to a head one day. I'd interviewed applicants nonstop throughout the morning, afternoon, and evening. I was trapped in my own office with applicants I knew would never be part of Systems & Space. In my own business, I was watching the clock, poised to escape as soon as it was five o'clock.

Just seconds away from five o'clock, moments before my escape, the agency called and said they had one more applicant they wanted me to interview. Nope, I'd had enough! There was no way I could endure even one more depressing interview. Certainly not after five o'clock.

Although I advised the agency that I'd had it for the day, they enthusiastically informed me, "She will be available after five o'clock tonight."

I was exhausted. After thinking about it, I concluded, "What the hell? I've been interviewing all day. I'll wait for her to show up."

Coincidentally, her name was also Emily—Emily Chin. From the moment she walked through our doors, she was sizing up Systems & Space. She cared about her surroundings and took an inventory of the staff and the excitement that was always evident in the office. Emily brought with her an aura of confidence. I felt it immediately.

She had been the controller of her family's roofing company. The similarities between the two businesses were remarkable: design, architecture, subassemblies, and installation. Her questions revealed a keen awareness of custom manufacturing. She explained that while she knew the requirements of a controller, she enjoyed the pace and the creativity of a manufacturing business. With that background and that attitude, I knew Emily would be a tremendous asset to Systems & Space. She would not just be crunching numbers. She would become a pivotal participant in our company's success.

Freeing myself from the burden of crunching numbers allowed me to inspire our team. It allowed me to be out in the field, developing new business. The equation was simple: volume equals profit, or volume equals loss. If your volume equals loss, you are enjoying life too much and not paying attention to what was necessary to sustain your enjoyment. Successful companies do not plateau. Industries change far too quickly for that. Plateaued enterprises are going in reverse; their owners just don't realize it yet.

Another critical point I learned is that you can control your effort and your time, but you cannot control the impact of the economy or political influences on your business or your clients' businesses. Therefore, you must be in control of yourself. The company must come first.

Bernie Huot, my mentor from Monroe Systems, taught me well. I often drew upon his influence during my early years: "You're not a sales manager until I see people coming to you with questions and you responding to them with the correct answers."

I was no longer a hopeful sales manager; I was now the owner of an expanding enterprise. More people than I'd imagined were coming to me with important questions that required precise answers. My answers were now affecting my employees' lives and the future of our corporation.

There were times, although not many, when I would forgo paying myself to ensure stability for my employees. These times were temporary, and there is almost no reason to mention them except to emphasize that the company always came first!

I was always aware of our numbers. I knew that at $3.5 million in sales, we were breaking even, covering expenses and payroll. At $5 million and above, we were generating a healthy amount of revenue. I also knew that as our volume increased, our costs stabilized. I could give my employees bonuses, thereby improving their living standards, but the increase was adding to our company's profit, not overhead!

Our payroll increased to thirty-two employees. These were hardworking, dedicated individuals who cared about one another and the product they were producing. We faced numerous challenges, including managing cash flow and navigating market fluctuations, but orchestrating a cohesive team allowed us to quickly address those difficulties and implement proper procedures to rectify any situation. Challenges were viewed as opportunities, and those opportunities became foundational in establishing a continuous improvement program. This program, which focused on learning from our experiences and making proactive changes, solidified our procedures and strengthened our position within the industry.

At Systems & Space, we didn't just design systems, engineer layouts, and construct them on location; we did so with an unwavering commitment to quality. Our in-house draftsman, proficient in engineering and computer-aided design (CAD) capabilities, allowed us to provide everything necessary for a competitive and accurate quotation.

Our commitment to delivering the highest quality in the industry has always been our driving force. This dedication to excellence ensures that Spacesaver products and Systems & Space service remain in a category of their own, providing our customers with the utmost confidence in our offerings.

As the business grew, so did our family life. Dana and Ryan enjoyed elementary school, and Janet and I enjoyed our membership at the Blackhawk Country Club. Between the children's school events and our club activities, we began making new friends and broadening our social circle. This growth in our personal lives mirrored the expansion of our business, and we found joy in both.

Family is everything; it always was. Although someone might consider my upbringing unconventional, it suited me perfectly. If my parents had raised me any other way, they would have limited me or altered my journey to success entirely. Balancing professional success with family values has always been my priority, and it's a key factor in my overall success.

Janet and I respected our kids at the same level our parents did us. We wanted them to recognize our unwavering belief and trust in them, so we gave them just enough distance and freedom to reveal their personalities and just enough parenting to protect them from the unnecessary consequences of bad decisions. This delicate balance was not always easy to maintain, but it was crucial in ensuring that our professional success did not come at the cost of our family's wellbeing.

As I think about it, I've got to laugh. When Ryan was still a child, I would drive him to school in my 1988 Porsche Turbo Carrera, which I had picked up for $25,000. It had a salvage title, and it looked and sounded the part. He'd always ask me to drop him off a few blocks from the school; he was happy to walk the rest of the way.

Two years later, I had an Aston Martin, followed by two Ferraris—a coupe and a convertible. Suddenly, Ryan wanted me to drop him off right in front of the school. He would have liked me to drop him off in the hallway if I could have done it! When I sold the coupe, I noticed that he seemed a bit downcast. I asked him if something was bugging him, and he said, "It was a lot cooler when you had two."

The kids' activities became the center of our lives. While I could find excitement in growing the business, my pride in my kids was overwhelming. Whether it was Dana's cheerleading, Ryan's T-ball and later lacrosse, or their shared experiences with their friends, engagement in their lives has been one of the most rewarding of my accomplishments. Many people have money. Many people have time. But few have both. The cars were great, but the investment in our kids' lives and the joy of seeing them grow into independent, flourishing adults is beyond any other measure of success.

Prosperity also allows one to fulfill other desires that are not often associated with success. One such desire is caring for the two people who brought you into the world. Being able to offer Mom and Dad the finest of living accommodations and the best of medical treatment—to show them that their patience and never-failing confidence in me paid off—was immeasurably fulfilling.

And then there's the extended family. I think about my first cousin, Alan Robinowitz, who is about fifteen years my junior, a close family member and friend. He had been a guard at the local jail, but he wanted more out of life. Alan and the jail's nurse practitioner, Scott Joyce, had become good friends. They shared the same desire for a better lifestyle and a more promising future.

They knew of a doctor in New Kensington, Pennsylvania, who started his own methadone clinic, a facility that provides medication-assisted treatment for individuals struggling with opioid addiction. It was evident to Alan and Scott from the doctor's car and clothes that he was making money. He would drive to the jail in Mercer, Pennsylvania, from New Kensington to administer methadone to inmates in need. It was a sixty-mile drive, about three hours on the road round-trip. My cousin and his friend saw an opportunity and opened a clinic closer to Mercer. Alan's clinic was small and relatively unknown; his competition was well-established.

One evening in January 2009, he called me. "Brad, I don't know what to do," he said. "My partner and I started this methadone clinic, but we only have fifty patients. There isn't enough cash flow to sustain it."

Alan was transparent with me. We discussed their debt, which had accumulated due to the high cost of medication and the low number of patients. I contacted my brother, Steve, who had become a successful accountant, and explained Alan's situation. I asked Steve to review the clinic's books to determine whether the business could be sustainable. Ever ready to assist, he audited the books and reported that everything was in order and clean. Alan and Scott simply lacked the capital. It would take $50,000 to $100,000 to cover the debt and put the clinic back on track.

Janet and I carefully considered the potential benefits and risks of collaboration with family. But Alan had already proven himself. We had unwavering faith in him and his mission. He was a man of integrity and purpose. If our financial support could help him achieve his goal, it was an investment we were more than willing to make.

By investing as a third partner with a one-third interest in the business, I was able to provide them with the financial resources they needed. And they've truly excelled! The ability to assist Alan in his time of need allowed me to contribute to a significant social mission and participate in his dream. Together, we achieved it: MISSION ACCOMPLISHED!

Just as I began to settle into a comfortable lifestyle, Mr. Kevin Carmody, the executive vice president at Krueger International (KI), called to add more "golden pavers" to my road to success.

"Brad, you don't know me yet, but I know you," he told me. "I've never met you, but I've heard you're really good. I've reviewed your numbers, and they support that claim. I'm not pleased with the current situation at our other West Coast locations. I'm going up to Sacramento and letting them know they are fucking gone!"

I understood him; he spoke my language.

Mr. Carmody continued, "So, after I meet you, I am going up there, firing those guys and dividing the business between you and San Francisco."

That's precisely what he did. With one strategic telephone call, our company's capacity more than doubled. This call led to my covering the entire East Bay down to Gilroy, over to Nevada, and up to but not including Napa, Sonoma. This left only the areas the San Francisco group covered, from San Francisco to Napa, Sonoma, and down to Monterey. But I had something no one else had. I had a desire to build an organization. I took on this responsibility with full awareness of its potential impact.

Taking over Sacramento presented me with a bonus: Andy! He'd been selling Spacesavers in Sacramento since Systems & Space moved to Pleasanton, and he moved to the Sacramento area. Just as it was when I stepped into Hercules and he was there to assist me with the transition, so it was as I took over the Sacramento territory. And Andy could sell.

You can't effectively tell someone how to sell or how to have an attractive personality. You cannot contrive authenticity. If it doesn't come naturally, it makes engaging with people much more difficult. There have been innumerable books written on how to sell, but for the most part, it is a gift. A person who has an engaging personality and wants to enjoy life is more magnetic.

To be a high-quality salesperson, you must be hungry. In my case, having a product that was, and still is, the best in its category increases that natural hunger to sell. But successful sales are also about self-control. Effective salespeople manage their enthusiasm and aggression. It is important to observe people and surroundings. Sales isn't constantly commanding the conversation. You cannot build a relationship or friendship by being the dominant person in the conversation. People like to hear themselves and their ideas verbalized. They want to see an interest, a positive response to their ideas. It is reaffirming; it shows respect.

Listening is a powerful tool in sales. When you listen intently, you show that you value what the potential client has to say. You build a foundation on which a lasting relationship can begin. Your responses to them are vitally important from the moment you meet. You must sell yourself before you can sell your product. Enter the potential client's office with the intention of building a friendship. The business will follow, but it all starts with listening.

Andy was a good man. He understood these principles of interaction and played an essential part in Systems & Space's success—until he confided in me that he had a divided allegiance. He was not moonlighting at another company. He had become fully invested in the world of politics and an avid advocate for a variety of issues facing California. Up until then, he'd managed the dual areas of commitment professionally. But then it happened.

You can't plan for some things, such as personal allegiances conflicting with professional responsibilities or the unexpected actions of trusted employees. These unforeseen challenges can significantly impact business operations.

One day, we shared a business luncheon with a very influential client. Andy was the salesperson servicing the account. It was a very upbeat, enthusiastic business meeting, and it ended as if we were all the best of friends and business partners.

Later that evening, during a television news broadcast, Andy was televised protesting against the same client's business. Needless to say, the conflict of interest did not go over well with our customer. The next morning, Andy and I discussed the situation. He was not only an employee; we were friends. We trusted each other's intentions and respected each other's endeavors. We felt mutually that he must choose between his employment and his political activism. He needed to follow where his heart was leading him. In 2017, after discussing his options, Andy said he was committed to pursuing political activism and had decided to resign from Systems & Space. It was a move I questioned and regretted, but noting how unconventional my life had also been, I had to respect his decision.

The foundational principles of our organization, personnel, and business flow were in place, tested, and refined to allow us to be duplicated wherever the opportunity presented itself for expansion. The Sacramento territory introduced Systems & Space to government business. Because of our presence in Sacramento, we began working with the branches of the United States military. Travis Air Force Base became a loyal customer of Systems & Space, a testament to our reliability.

Occasionally, you meet competent individuals who don't have the hunger to build an organization. They are prepared to run high-margin profit centers, but they may fail to establish the necessary infrastructure to achieve a thriving business, including warehouse space, installers, office personnel, and salespeople. Other opportunities begin to blur their original intentions, and their company begins to falter.

Such was the case in San Francisco. Like most industries, ours is very small; there are no secrets. Disgruntled employees contact other distributors, and you can get a reasonably accurate picture of what is taking place within their business. It's the same product line, mind you, but a different business philosophy, one that prioritizes short-term gains over long-term growth.

I would never entertain the thought of hiring someone from a different location unless they'd moved out of that territory and had no influence within it, had an excellent reputation, and had a track record of success. If I could help them better themselves and see them as an asset to our team, I would extend the opportunity. When you experience numerous individuals from a single location inquiring about working for your business, it is an obvious sign that the company isn't performing well. A deeper business review, which involves analyzing sales data, team performance, and innovation levels, usually reveals declining sales, a lack of innovation, and a demotivated team.

Bob Russo and Rebecca Horne owned System Concepts, the San Francisco arm of Spacesavers' western distribution. As a fellow business owner in the same industry, I would meet them for lunch every couple of months at Scott's Seafood in Jack London Square. They were good people. I enjoyed getting together with them and discussing the business climate our two companies were experiencing. We openly shared some of our actions to address the ebb and flow of business throughout the Bay Area. My gut told me that Bob and Rebecca were not having fun. They were highly talented individuals, but their talents appeared to be misdirected. Bob was a stellar high-level salesperson. There was no reason for him to be making deliveries in his van if he'd built an organization. Rebecca's attention seemed to be drawn to Colorado. Neither was in a position to fulfill who they were and what they wanted to achieve.

On Friday, August 5, 2011, Bob, Rebecca, and I met at Scott's Seafood Restaurant, but this luncheon would be unlike our previous ones. There were few pleasantries shared, and there was very little idle chatter. We sat down. I looked across the table at the two of them.

"You're in trouble, aren't you?" I asked.

At first, they played it cool. No one wants to admit when the challenge has become too big and their preparations were too small.

I broke the awkward silence by recognizing and addressing their business challenges. "Look, I'm here to listen to whatever you have to say. Whatever it is, it is alright with me, but I know you are in trouble. So, what's your number?"

"We are down," Rebecca responded. "We are down a lot."

I said, "Okay, look. I will cut you a check for half of your debt today and the other half a year from now. You will be free and clear, with no loss and no more pressure."

The paperwork was done within twenty-four hours. On Saturday, August 9, 2011, I purchased complete control and ownership of the Northern California territory.

In Loving Memory

ROBERT M. LIEBER "HOUSECAT"

MHS
CLASS OF 1968

SON, BROTHER, FRIEND, VETERAN,
STEELWORKER, AVID READER

Enjoy Reading

Top Left: My late brother Bob "Housecat" Lieber

Top Right: The dedication plaque at the Monessen Public Library Reading Room

Lower Left: Cousin Rick Lieber, Brother, Steve Lieber, and me

Lower Right: Steve, Cousin Alan Robinowitz, and me

From the Lieber Family Album

Chapter 13
Trips with Friends

J anet and I have cherished many vacations with our friends, each
one a testament to the importance of our relationships. Whether
we journeyed with a large group, with a few couples, or with just
Janet and me on those rare, intimate trips, each adventure was a
reminder of the blessings we share with our family and friends.

And there were the cruises, too many to mention, except for two.
One of them took place around the year 2000. You'll recall that when I
committed to purchasing the Hercules territory, on my flight home I
made a list of ten essential things I had to accomplish. Years had gone
by, and there remained one important item I'd failed to correct. One
thing continued to plague me day in and day out. Yes, it's true. I now
controlled all the territories in Northern California. Yes, Systems &
Space was a tremendous success. Yes, we were traveling the world and
enjoying every moment of it. But there was one more critical endeavor
that could no longer be delayed.

On this trip, we were vacationing with Scott and Kim Archibald. It
was a stunningly beautiful Caribbean cruise. We'd been on many
before, but this one was especially beautiful. The food, drink, entertain-
ment, and sunsets all seemed more fulfilling.

I excused myself from the group and went to the onboard hair-stylist's shop.

"I want you to take it all off. Shave my head!" I said forcefully.

"Sir, I—I don't want to shave your head. Are you serious?" the young stylist stammered.

"I've been living with this for too many years now. If I don't do it now, I never will." My tone of voice must have shaken her into an awareness that somehow, perhaps by fate, she had been chosen to accomplish a long-suppressed desire.

"Sit down. Let's get this done!" Her sudden enthusiasm caused me to have second thoughts momentarily. Nevertheless, we accomplished the deed. And, I'll be damned, I looked good! I put my ball cap on and returned to our suite. I kept my hat on while Janet and I got ready to meet Scott and Kim in their suite.

I waited for the right moment to remove my cap. Scott, Kim, and Janet had already begun conversing. No one knew I had been contemplating such a bold move, not even Janet. No one gave me a second look —until I removed my hat. Their conversation ended—abruptly! Scott's eyes widened, Kim's jaw dropped, but Janet remained unfazed. At the outset she might have been amused, but she knew me and was always ready for anything. It was as if she was thinking, "Oh well, that's Brad."

After a brief moment of nervous laughter, everyone realized how much they liked it. And I liked it too. It was like I'd been redeemed; I had accomplished everything on my list. Now I could enjoy the vacation!

The second cruise was an eight-day, seven-night New Year's extravaganza on Royal Caribbean Lines. There were three couples on this cruise: Janet and me, Scott and Kim Archibald, and Tim and Cammy Cox. Tim and Cammy's son, Matt, and his friend, Chris, joined us. Everyone enjoyed the celebration and their time together. The trip was everything you would hope for in such a vacation: beautiful skies, smooth sailing, relaxing dinners, and fabulous service. It was a fantastic way to ring in 2005!

We didn't see much of the boys on that trip. Tim, however, found out what they had been doing when it came time to clear their bar tab. They'd had $4,500 worth of fun! Tim remained calm, cool, and collected, but he continues to talk about it decades later.

Reflecting on my journey, it's fascinating to see how many influences from my childhood have shaped my adulthood. Pat Herron's 1962 candy apple red split window 427 Corvette and Chevelle 396 were two such influences. With their sleek designs and powerful engines, these cars ignited my love for automobiles at a young age. And that love has only grown stronger over the years.

In total, I have owned seven Ferraris. I now own an F12 with a red exterior and a black interior and an 812 GTS red exterior, black interior convertible. Why Ferraris? They are beautiful, fast, and a testament to their designers' and engineers' technical and artistic genius—and they are fun!

The annual Ferrari Rally, a luxurious event organized by Emmanuel Turin of Ferrari of San Francisco, further enhances our love for our cars. This exclusive rally, attended by customers of the dealership, is a true indulgence. Scott and Kim Archibald also transport their vehicle to the rally locations. We have made friends with six other couples who attend, and we enjoy the five-star accommodations and restaurants selected for our comfort and enjoyment.

Before the rally, our cars undergo a thorough service and detailing process. The result? They look and sound as if they just rolled off the assembly line. Carriers then transport them to the rally location. It is a five-day journey covering 225 to 275 miles daily. After each day's ride, the cars are once again serviced and detailed, ensuring they are in top condition for the next day's adventure.

It has become a greatly anticipated event for the car owners and the communities that host them. The destinations have included Sedona, Arizona; Santa Fe, New Mexico; Yellowstone, Wyoming; Deer Valley, Utah; and Vail, Colorado.

Chapter 14
Recognizing Talent

Golf remains a steadfast companion through all seasons. Whether in the company of others or savoring a solitary round, the game's allure never wanes, offering a sense of continuity and timelessness.

My dad introduced me to golf when I was twelve; it's a memory I hold dear. On the golf course, it was just Dad and me, and our bond grew stronger with every swing of the club. The lessons he imparted about both the game and life are ones I carry with me to this day, continuing to inspire personal growth and reflection.

My game hasn't changed much when you consider the number of years I've enjoyed it. To paraphrase a quote from the great Arnold Palmer, I can honestly say that having played golf for many years and having had the pleasure of playing golf in some of the world's most spectacular locations—Pinehurst, Pebble Beach, Spyglass—I've gotten older!

The funny thing about golf is you can't win or lose unless you are a professional player; you can only play the game. You can place high stakes on a round with your buddies, but the money circles back in time. When all is said and done, it is the game.

In 1994, shortly after moving from Southern California, I began playing golf at Canyon Lakes Golf Course, an 18-hole public course in

San Ramon. The course was nestled in a picturesque valley, and when the sun set behind the hills, it cast a golden hue over the greens. It was there that I met twin brothers Mike and Mark Mazzocco. We played together every weekend, sharing stories and laughter amid the serene beauty of the course.

Joining the Blackhawk Country Club in 1995 opened the door to two stunning championship courses. I found myself on the greens three to four times a week. It was through my son's activities at the Creative Learning Center that I met Scott Archibald. Ryan became friends with Scott's son, Bryant. Soon, our families were introduced through their relationship and united by the game of golf. Scott and his wife, Kim, were also members at Blackhawk Country Club, as were Tim and Cammy Cox. As our friendships developed, we began taking golf trips and vacations together. Sometimes the six of us would travel together; other times, it would just be two couples. But we always had fun. We shared more than just a love for golf; we shared life's ups and downs. Our shared experiences on the course—the victories and defeats, the laughter and camaraderie—formed a bond that transcended the game itself.

There was a young assistant golf pro at Blackhawk Country Club who stood out from the other employees. I'd been playing for four or five years, and over that time, Jordan Jaime and I built a friendly relationship that added to the pleasure of the game. Everyone enjoyed Jordan. He possessed a welcoming professionalism that was genuine and infectious. He projected a keen awareness of the Blackhawk members' needs and was always ready to assist with a smile. I liked this kid and looked forward to visiting him whenever I checked in.

I truly came to understand who he was on a potentially chaotic day. It was 6:30 a.m., and the course was first-come, first-serve. Jordan was the sole Blackhawk Country Club employee on site. The employee responsible for bringing golf carts around for members, removing their golf bags from their cars, and situating them appropriately on their assigned carts was absent. But when others did not show up, Jordan did. His ability to handle stress was impressive as he seamlessly managed the situation.

Jordan welcomed us, checked us in, politely excused himself to retrieve our cart, situated our bags, let us know the flag positions on the course, and wished us a fantastic game without ever acknowledging there was any challenge. I'd witnessed his professionalism for years, but at that moment, my eyes were opened to his character. His unwavering commitment to service and his ability to gracefully and efficiently handle a potentially stressful situation were truly inspiring. There was no doubt in my mind I had to hire him. I didn't know what I would do with him, but he had to be part of the Systems & Space team.

I didn't approach Jordan that day but waited until a few days later when the clubhouse was not crowded, and he was not involved with any members.

"Good morning, Jordan," I enthusiastically called with a wave.

"Good morning, Mr. Lieber," he replied.

Never one to waste time, I asked, "Hey, Jordan. Would you be interested in talking to me about coming to work for us?"

He did not appear to be caught off guard. He was unflappable, another essential character trait. Jordan smiled and politely replied, "Let me think about it."

From previous interactions, I knew that friends had approached him about working with them in Stockton. These families owned hundreds of acres of walnut groves and lived an enviable lifestyle. However, he was not one to take a job simply for the sake of it. He was strategic in his career choices, always thinking about his future and how to achieve wealth.

A day or two later, Jordan expressed his interest in talking more seriously about my question and visiting Systems & Space. We set up a visit for a week later. I watched him as he entered the building. His entrance was not unlike my memory of Emily Chin's entrance, taking in everything around him. He asked the right questions, the kind that would be asked by someone who had invested time in determining who they were, where they fit, and how they could become successful.

Two weeks after his visit, I formally offered him a job. I still didn't know what that would be. I already had six sales planners. Was there room for another planner? Yes. Was another necessary? Probably not.

We sent Jordan back to Fort Atkinson, Wisconsin, for training at Spacesaver Headquarters. He returned a week later, bubbling with excitement. Witnessing this phenomenal organization in person affects everyone the same way, as they come to know, beyond a shadow of a doubt, that they have an opportunity to build wealth and enjoy all of their dreams.

It was around the same time that Systems & Space suffered an unplanned, unfortunate transition. As I mentioned earlier, personnel challenges can arise from inflated egos. Such was the case of an employee I'd worked with for twenty-five years.

No one is irreplaceable. With his dismissal, most of his responsibilities were assumed by dedicated employees who were eager to contribute to the future of the company and achieve personal and financial growth.

His leaving closely coincided with Jordan's hiring. I realized that, while many of his responsibilities were absorbed by others, one area of our business was left without oversight. That area was our VAR—Value-Added Reseller. Granted, it was a big responsibility. The program is a market that is only for resale. Systems & Space works with furniture dealers such as Steelcase, Haworth Office Furniture, AllSteel Office Furniture, and others like them who introduce us to their customers as specialists. We do all the design, project management, and installation just like we do for any other customer, except that the office furniture companies buy it from us and bundle it with their projects for their customers. I'd always envisioned it becoming a significant revenue stream, but it never seemed to take off.

I wondered whether I should give the responsibility to Jordan. The previous employee had accomplished nothing of note with VAR. Would it be discouraging to saddle a new employee with an unproven, currently unprofitable business segment? Then, I realized—it was

Jordan Jaime I would be handing it to. We hadn't yet seen what the possibilities might be.

Jordan shadowed each of the six planners, all of whom made every effort to ensure his success. That's the environment at Systems & Space. Everyone is looking out for each other's best interests. Michael Byard, who heads up our CAD and Estimation, and Jordan hit it off well, ensuring he would become proficient in those important areas.

Jordan, who had been an assistant golf pro, and Emily, whose son, Alex, was on the golf team at the University of San Francisco, quickly established a unique relationship. This is just one example of the warmth and inclusivity that define our company culture. Emily always made certain that everyone in the company had the tools and information they required to fulfill their responsibilities.

Chapter 15
Change

Time has a way of introducing circumstances that alter our perspectives, goals, and values. The passage of time influences our lifestyles, requiring us to adapt. What was once a primary focus becomes an occasional source of enjoyment. As we get older, our children get older, and they begin having children of their own. Their needs change, and our responsibilities shift from guiding them and shaping their lives to participating in the lives they have established.

Systems & Space was now a well-established, highly regarded organization. I was proud of the company. It was like a child I'd raised to full maturity. I knew that for the business to maintain healthy growth, I would need to begin entertaining the thought of stepping aside and retiring. It wasn't a possibility I dreaded. The idea of selling it and retiring added to the sense of accomplishment. To have erected a corporation that others within the industry recognized, that a private equity group wished to be involved with, and that competitors admired brought satisfaction and a sense of completion.

As mentioned earlier, you do not rush into selling a thriving corporation. For the better part of a decade, I'd quietly been talking with a group of investors interested in Systems & Space. I hadn't been looking to sell anytime soon. It was my due diligence in preparation for the future.

Little did I realize how quickly the future was sneaking up on me.

There was just enough time to sneak in one last round of golf before taking Janet on a week-long vacation in Cancun. Our trips there or to Cabo San Lucas were a yearly respite. Both Janet and I were looking forward to it. Over the years, we'd become acquainted with many of the restaurateurs and artisans in Cabo, and it had become a home away from home.

The morning was unusually cool at Blackhawk Country Club. It made us even more eager for our trip to Cancun. Scott Archibald, Dale Miller, Don Cavianco, and I were playing the Falls Course. We were on the 453-yard sixth hole, a par five. I'd taken my second shot and pushed it to the right of the bunker. Scott had a beautiful second shot, right down the center of the fairway. I would have had a nice shot—if it hadn't careened off the toe of my club.

I drove my golf cart to the bunker but couldn't find my ball. I glanced in the trap to see if it had somehow taken a bad bounce and gone in, but it was nowhere in sight. I'd watched it leave the club and go to the right. It should have been right there in plain sight.

"Brad, what ya doing?" Scott asked as he came up to me.

"I can't find my ball," I replied, confused. "I hit it right over here, but I can't find it."

"What are you talking about?" Scott said. "It's right here."

I walked to where he was standing but could not immediately see my ball.

"What are you doing, Brad? It's right in front of you." Scott shook his head and chuckled as I floundered, trying to focus on my golf ball and take a third swing. But something was wrong. Nothing about my swing felt natural. I was hacking at the ball as if hoeing weeds. I had the sensation I'd never swung a club before, and it had come on suddenly.

After the sixth hole, I told the fellas I would sit the next hole out because I wasn't feeling well. I didn't recognize it as something I had felt before. I ended up sitting in the cart for the next three holes.

"Fellas, I'm not feeling well. I'm going to call it a day and go home and rest," I announced.

They each wished me well, but Scott was especially concerned. He asked me again how I was. He knew me well, and this was not like me. I tried to brush him off by telling him I would be fine. I just needed to get some rest.

Janet was surprised when I walked through the door.

"What are you doing home so early? Didn't you play?" she asked.

"Ah, I wasn't feeling well," I responded. "I'm going to watch the Steelers-Raiders game."

I fell asleep during the game and can't remember who won. Janet woke me up to ask about dinner, and I suggested we order takeout. She brought the Chinese takeout menu from the kitchen and handed it to me. A strange sensation came over me: deep confusion. Looking at the menu, I could tell the difference between the Chinese characters and the English letters, but I could not understand either. The words written in English made no sense. I knew I should understand them, but it was like deciphering a puzzle. I looked up at Janet, my confusion and fear clearly visible.

"What is it, Brad? What's wrong?" There was desperation in her voice.

I just looked at her. Not only could I not read the menu, but I could not vocalize a response. Janet ran to the telephone and called my doctor, Dr. Bela Kenessey, who instructed Janet to get me to the emergency room immediately. Janet took me to San Ramon Regional Hospital, where the emergency room personnel wasted no time initiating their rapid response protocol.

I'd suffered a stroke.

The hospital staff were unable to determine the extent of damage the stroke might have caused. Timing is critical for stroke patients, and I'd casually driven through three additional holes at the golf course, gone home, and taken in the better part of the Steelers game. The doctors there did all they could to stabilize my vital signs before transferring me to Eden Hospital in Castro Valley. There, the neuroscience staff saw me.

The doctors determined that the accumulation of plaque blocked my carotid arteries. I needed to be stabilized for a few more days before they would perform the surgery to remove the plaque. I asked the doctor if I would live, expecting a hearty, "We'll have you up and about in no time!"

Instead, the doctor soberly responded, "Mr. Lieber, I don't know."

It was one of the first times I'd ever experienced fear. The realization that my body could betray me in such a way was a profound shock. The uncertainty about the future and whether I'd be able to return to my everyday life was overwhelming.

I called Emily. She needed to know what was going on. The trip to Cancun was canceled, but since everyone at Systems & Space knew I would be gone for a week, there was no need to tell them the real reason I was not in the office.

We waited until I was supposed to have returned from Cancun to call the team together and let them know about my stroke. Janet came with me to the office, which tipped off several of the team members to the fact that something was not quite right.

There wasn't much to tell. Janet and I still didn't know what damage the lapse in time before getting medical help might have caused. So far, I seemed fine. After the surgery, it would take six weeks of recovery before returning to my routine. The recovery process was challenging, both physically and emotionally. Someone would have to remain with me during the two-week interim period before my surgery. The support of my loved ones was crucial during this time.

The weeks following my successful surgery gave me time to reevaluate my life. The experience put into perspective the importance of every moment. For the first time in my life, I faced my mortality. My stroke was an unanticipated circumstance that I needed to address with the same positive attitude I'd had while building my business.

This event brought back the somber memory of Ed Stern's death and the unimaginable dilemma Linda, his wife, had faced. She'd suffered the paralyzing shock of her husband's sudden death, and without adequate time to mourn, was forced to take on the tremendous responsibility of running an organization she knew very little about. I remembered vowing then that I would never put Janet in such a position. I immediately called the private equity group I'd casually visited with and told them I was ready to talk more earnestly about the sale of Systems & Space. I always knew I would one day sell my business. When the time actually came, the words seemed foreign coming from my lips.

Our formal discussions began in 2019. Emily was the only person who was aware of my decision to sell. As our controller, she had our numbers, our company profile, and the specific financials the investors wanted to review.

They reviewed the business for a year. Emily provided full disclosure of our numbers during that period to assist in a smooth transition should the sale occur as planned. Then, they provided me with their business plan. It was as if I'd been hit in the face with ice water.

Their business plan was unacceptable for the company I'd raised, the employees I'd hired and worked with, and the customers I'd served. They intended to split our entire roster of employees into thirds. The bottom third would be fired. The second third would be groomed to gain proficiency and productivity to join the top tier. Anyone within the second group who could not make the adjustment would also be removed from the roster of employees.

I knew these people. I knew their talents and their commitment to Systems & Space. I'd seen them grow. I'd witnessed second-generation employees following in their family members' footsteps, like in the steel mills during my childhood in Monessen. These workers and their families benefited from solid employment and opportunities to advance. This was not just a business; this was a family. No! No amount of money would cause me to betray the loyalty these men and women had shown over the years. I called my attorney, and the sale was off. There would be no further discussion.

When I invited Emily to my office and disclosed the unexpected turn of events, her reaction was one of thoughtful contemplation. She was not indifferent, but rather reserved in expressing her emotions until she fully grasped the implications. Emily's approach to her role as the controller of Systems & Space was akin to a proprietor, always acting in the best interest of the company's employees and the corporation's future.

I informed Emily that I needed some time to reorganize my thoughts. There was indeed a Plan B, a strategic contingency that I had kept to myself until I had exhausted all avenues with the private equity group. The submission of their business plan effectively made the decision for me.

The following day, Emily approached me. She'd been reading my mind, something I'd already been convinced she was capable of doing. She asked if I would ever consider selling the company to her—which happened to be my Plan B. We sat down and began a new line of discussion that would result in one of the most significant decisions of my career.

"Emily, you're going to need a partner," I said.

We discussed several individuals, but only one caught our attention: Jordan Jaime. After taking charge of our Value-Added Reseller program, he transformed it from virtually nothing to a program that generated an impressive three to five million dollars in added revenue.

But Emily valued the company and the established Systems & Space family too highly to make a rash decision.

"Brad, Jordan lives in Sacramento," she pointed out. "That's 100 miles away. Let's put him to the test. Let's tell him we need his presence in Pleasanton several times a week. We'll find out his level of commitment."

When I made the call to Jordan, he didn't even blink. Just as he was ready to serve in whatever capacity was necessary when I first met him at Blackhawk Country Club, he was prepared to do whatever it took to make Systems & Space a better company. All the while, he had no idea he was being considered for a partnership in the company. That's character!

It only took Emily and me a month or two to be convinced. We already had the best possible partnership in place, one built on trust and commitment. It was only appropriate that we let Jordan know.

I'd watched these two individuals work together during the period I was negotiating a potential sale. Emily's knowledge, work ethic, and considerate heart reminded me of Janet's father, LeRoy Golman. Jordan, a hardworking visionary who is always positive, leads by example, assesses situations, and makes decisions, reminded me of myself. Emily and Jordan were my Plan B. Emily would oversee administration and finance, and Jordan would oversee sales.

My proposal was brief and to the point.

"Emily, Jordan, if you are interested, I would like the two of you to purchase Systems & Space."

They looked at each other and then back at me. Of course, selling to a group of investors would have been easy. We would agree on a price, cut a check, and be done with it. I knew working out the details of a sale to Emily and Jordan would require more creativity. I was up for the task if they would take it up with me.

They would need to secure a loan from the Small Business Administration, and it would take six to nine months to complete the loan process. No one saw any possible roadblocks. It was smooth sailing, a done deal—until it wasn't.

They were applying for a federal SBA loan. The SBA found one customer on our books who was dealing in cannabis. We were not involved with any portion of their product line (although I did find it humorous, considering my early years in Monessen). Systems & Space sold them shelving. Because of this association, at the very last minute, the SBA pulled the loan. While the pens were in Emily and Jordan's hands, ready to close the deal with their signatures, it all ended.

We all knew that this partnership was the right thing. I reasoned that if this were to have gone smoothly, it would have been contrary to everything I'd ever experienced in my business journey. It had to be unconventional to be genuinely in keeping with my story.

Within two weeks, I assured Emily and Jordan that I would handle the details to ensure the transition worked out for everyone. I didn't need to change the people; I only had to modify the process of getting them to the finish line.

Emily and Jordan made it clear that there would be one irrevocable condition: there would never be another President of Systems & Space. They bestowed upon me the honor of retaining the titles of founder and president emeritus.

Taking friends on a gold outing.
L to R: Don Cabianco, Bill McMurray, Scott Archibald, me, Dale Miller, John Peterson, Tim Cox, and Carl Manna

Right: An event with Scott and Kim Archibald

Below: An event with Tim and Cammy Cox

Family Photographs

Chapter 16
Leaving Grand River Academy

As Janet and I strolled from the dormitory to the main building of Grand River Academy, I couldn't help but feel the weight of the memories I'd cherished for so long. These were not just fleeting recollections, but a significant part of my journey that I was revisiting.

We thanked Holly and Thomas for their hospitality.

"You know, it's a rare and special occasion when our former students return," Holly remarked.

"Well, when I recognized all the signs driving from the airport, and I mentioned to Janet we had to be close, she insisted we make the trip," I responded. "And I am so glad we did."

We said our goodbyes and began our drive back to Meadville.

"That was nice," Janet remarked.

The flood of memories was so intense that I was momentarily lost in them, unable to respond immediately.

Janet recognized my contemplative expression. "Wasn't that nice, Brad? Aren't you glad we came?"

I was at a loss for words to express the emotional impact our visit to the school had on me.

"Janet, it was unbelievable!"

Now, as I sit in my office reminiscing, having passed on the torch of

Systems & Space to capable hands, I am not just content but deeply fulfilled. The work we've done and the impact we've had on our employees give me a profound sense of accomplishment that I carry with me always.

Despite some of my early years of aimlessness and what others might have thought was lacking in my preparation, my life has soared beyond my wildest expectations, reaching heights I never imagined.

And I'm still having fun!

Above: Jordan Jaime, me, and Emily Chin

Below: Admiring the accomplishments

Epilogue

To write an autobiography, you have to have lived a book. You must have allowed yourself to experience life, not in the shadow of another man or woman's story, but in your own moments. These unique experiences shape our stories and make them worth sharing, offering encouragement and validation to others.

Success isn't typically born from the actions of those who simply conform to societal norms or adhere to the expectations of others. Most books on success are written to highlight the journeys of others who dared to be different. These individuals, like me, have taken risks, faced ridicule, embraced struggles, and focused on their goals with unwavering commitment. Over time, the repeated actions of these people evolve into principles of success, inspiring hope in others and motivating those who hear their stories.

I don't view myself as having achieved anything out of the ordinary. Instead, I've lived my own narrative. Like many other "originals," my story is a blend of survival and aspiration. It is defined by overcoming challenges and striving for personal growth and success.

Years ago, when Sean Corrigan, president of Rockpoint Capital Ltd., suggested I write a book, I didn't realize I was already living it.

What about you? What will you contribute to society that could serve as the unconventional key to someone else's success? I encourage you to live your story!

Brad Lieber

Glossary of Success Principles

Brad Lieber's journey is not solely for your enjoyment, but, ironically, it is for your education. Each experience, each moment of joy, contains hidden success principles. It's up to you to find them. Remember, success is not something that aggressively seeks a candidate. Instead, success passively awaits those who aggressively pursue it.

1. Be hungry.
2. Surround yourself with things that inspire you.
3. Be honest with yourself, your virtues, and your challenges.
4. Avoid fitting patterns designed by others.
5. Be observant.
6. Diversify profitability.
7. You don't need to be appreciated by everyone.
8. Be appreciated by those who make a difference.
9. Be creative.
10. Consider the positive and the negative possibilities.
11. EMBRACE THE RISK.
12. Don't waste your imagination on small dreams.
13. Take time to live and enjoy the present.
14. Find humor in unconventional places.

15. Accept change as a new adventure.
16. Build friendships.
17. Admit failures and then move on.
18. Values are the foundation upon which you build.
19. Be aware of those you encounter.
20. Look beyond the present. Your decision might impact others for generations to come.
21. Always be fair.
22. Be you. You are the best version of yourself
23. Embrace change as a welcomed motivator.
24. It's okay to change your mind.
25. You need not adopt other people's problems.
26. Take breaks.
27. Never be jealous. Embrace another's success as your encouragement.
28. Make big moves.
29. Show up!
30. Believe, and feed your belief with optimism!
31. Do the work.
32. You don't need to know everything.
33. Understand what you need to know and work.
34. Compete with what you know you can achieve.
35. Never fully know what you can achieve.
36. You'll need to give something up to live something better.
37. Be willing to walk away.
38. You are not a leader until you help others get where they cannot go alone.
39. Create wealth, not a bank account.
40. Build a business, not a hobby.
41. Set your boundaries.
42. Always set high expectations for those who work for you.
43. Identify unmet needs and fill them.
44. Create expansion.
45. Invite others into the process.

46. Reward the successes of others with sincere congratulations.
47. Prioritize your customers' needs
48. Practice common sense.
49. Don't invest more time thinking about something than it is worth.
50. It doesn't hurt to listen to a proposal even if, at first, it isn't what you were looking for.
51. Sometimes you have to be humble.
52. Sometimes you have to be proud.
53. Know the difference in those times.
54. Be direct, don't pull punches.
55. You carry a family name. Honor it with your character.
56. Success is not defined by accumulated wealth.
57. Be successful in living.
58. Persevere.
59. Accept and share your recognition.
60. Average people do the work.
61. Successful people do whatever it takes.
62. An average person will never be successful.
63. Listening is your most powerful tool.
64. Successful businesses are collaborative movements of engaged individuals committed to doing their best and sharing each other's successes.
65. Businesses are continually evolving; so are successful people.
66. Your employees have the power to hire and fire themselves, but you maintain the power to inform them of their decision.
67. Know your numbers and stay ahead of them.
68. Timing is everything, but you have to show up.
69. You may have to stay after hours.
70. Free yourself to do what you do best.
71. Reward yourself—reward yourself BIG.

72. Reward others, never beyond what they deserve, always beyond what they expect.
73. Keep looking for opportunities.
74. Be authentic.
75. Never lose your hunger.
76. Manage your enthusiasm and aggression.
77. You cannot build a relationship by dominating the conversation.
78. Do not invest time in someone unwilling to invest time in themselves.
79. Never compromise your integrity.
80. When in doubt, go with your gut. You can always change your mind.
81. Enjoy time away from work; value friendships.
82. Find value in quiet times, quiet reflection.
83. Look for talent in others; observe them when no one knows you are watching.
84. When in doubt, play a round of golf.
85. Always have a plan B.
86. Take care of your health.
87. Make things happen.
88. Be grateful.
89. Let others edify you and say, "Thank you."
90. Write a book to inspire others when you have achieved beyond your dreams.

About the Author

Brad Lieber, the founder and president emeritus of Systems & Space, Incorporated, took an unconventional path to success, defying the typical norms associated with wealth and achievement. He put it this way:

"I always believed my path would be paved with gold. It didn't take long for me to realize that I would be on my hands and knees paving it."

Resilience in the face of challenges enabled Brad to pave his path to success. His story shows that success is an achievable result of one's determination, passion, and perseverance, rather than a product of formal education and adherence to conventional paths.

Brad did not have any formal education to speak of and did not invest his time reading success books; you would never find him in the self-help section of a library. Instead, he learned from real-life experiences and the people around him. Motivated by individuals who embodied the lifestyle he aspired to, Brad believed that their education was not the key to achieving that lifestyle. He was determined to discover that special "something" that would lead to his success.

Brad maintained an unwavering orientation toward success, allowing opportunities and hard work to fill the gaps. For him, selling is not an academic subject but an art form made of genuine connections with people. Brad understands that selling involves befriending others and making it easy for them to acquire what they need and desire. It is about becoming a gateway to their dreams and desires.

"You can't teach someone how to sell, have a personality, build rapport, and encourage people to use your services," he said. "If it doesn't come naturally, selling becomes much more challenging. Generally speaking, people do not want to be sold to; they want to make great purchases—there's a significant difference! A person with natural charisma, who enjoys life, tends to be more magnetic. Whether male or female, that individual can be successful if provided with a quality product to sell, if they have the hunger to succeed."

Brad possesses an insatiable appetite for success, which he shares with those involved in his remarkable enterprise. His passion for life is contagious, inspiring those around him to strive for their best.

This book offers a chance to witness, up close and personal, one man's remarkable journey and the lives he touched through his achievements. Brad's success not only benefited him; it also inspired and empowered those around him. His enterprise has become a platform for others to achieve their dreams, and his story continues to motivate and guide aspiring entrepreneurs.

www.ingramcontent.com/pod-product-compliance
Lightning Source LLC
Chambersburg PA
CBHW071759120626

46550CB00002B/849